Growing Proteas

Rob McLennan

Kangaroo Press

About the author

Rob McLennan was born and raised in country Victoria and developed a strong interest in gardening and a love of the Australian bush at an early age.

He later graduated from the University of Melbourne with a Bachelor of Science and a Diploma of Education. He is a keen gardener and a member of the Society for Growing Australian Plants with his main interest being the Australian members of the Proteaceae family.

Currently he is a full-time secondary college teacher of science, maths and horticulture. He and his wife Claire also run a small wholesale protea nursery and cut flower business.

Acknowledgments

The author would like to acknowledge the huge contribution to this book of his wife Claire. She not only word processed the text but also managed to keep the children busy at the same time.

He is also very grateful to Margot Waters for the outstanding floral arrangements.

Cover: *Protea eximia*

Reprinted 1995
First published in 1993 by Kangaroo Press Pty Ltd
3 Whitehall Road Kenthurst NSW 2156 Australia
P.O. Box 6125 Dural Delivery Centre NSW 2158
Printed in Hong Kong through Colorcraft Ltd

ISBN 0 86417 499 3

Contents

1 Introduction

Proteas have become one of the most popular and widely grown garden shrubs in recent years. Also, large commercial plantings have been established to supply the cut flower market. Despite this, very few books are available to provide information on their cultivation, especially in a format readily accessible to the average keen gardener.

The main aim of this book is to attempt to provide as much useful and practical information as possible to anyone wishing to grow their own proteas. Obviously with such an enormous plant family it is impossible to cover all the species and all the hybrids now available, but most of the more common or easily obtainable protea species have been included. Any new protea hybrids will generally show very similar characteristics to the parent species and the general rules for cultivation and management will be the same.

The Protea Family

The plants commonly called proteas are a small group belonging to the enormous ancient plant family Proteaceae. This family also includes the subfamily Grevilleoideae of which the most well known genera are the Australian banksias, grevilleas and macadamias, and is one of the dominant southern hemisphere plant families.

In this book the most common members of the plant tribe Proteae are looked at in detail, that is, the *Protea* species, *Leucadendron* species and *Leucospermum* species. These are all native to southern Africa.

THE FAMILY TREE

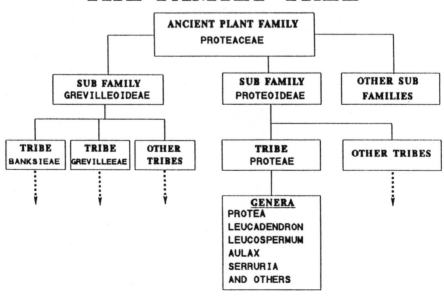

4

Why Grow Proteas?

Proteas are such a diverse group of plants that there would seem to be a protea for every garden site or purpose.

They show the whole range of growth habits. Some proteas and leucadendons make beautiful groundcovers or low rockery plants. There are many medium-sized proteas for use as feature plants or in mixed garden beds. Others grow to large bushy shrubs or small trees useful for beautiful windbreaks or as screening plants.

The range of protea, leucadendron and leucospermum colours covers almost the whole spectrum from creams to greens, through a range of pinks to vibrant reds.

Proteas can also withstand long dry periods and have generally proved easy to grow and disease resistant given reasonable drainage and plenty of sun.

The added bonus is that proteas can also be grown for profit on a small or large scale, as they are one of the most popular cut flowers world wide for floral art or floristry. Protea flowers and foliage are renowned for their extremely long vase life and strong straight stems making them the ideal cut flower.

The Flowers

Protea 'flowers' are really a combination of coloured *bracts* surrounding a mass of individual *florets* which make up the central flower mass. Bracts are actually modified leaves.

The leucadendrons have male and female 'flowers'. The female flower has the cone, the male flower produces the pollen. These central flower parts are surrounded by coloured bracts which are less numerous then the protea bracts, usually smaller and much more open.

Leucospermum 'flowers' are made up of a mass of prominent styles above a lower mass of perianths. The styles being above the pollen producers encourages cross-pollination between plants. The bracts on leucospermums are insignificant and found low on the flower head.

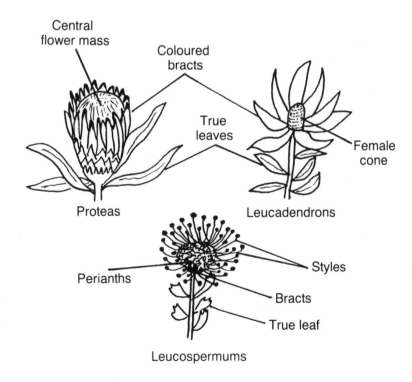

The flowers

2 Growing Proteas

Choosing Suitable Proteas

There is surely a protea to suit every type of garden. However a little thought and planning before buying your protea plants will go a long way toward making the right choice for your particular needs. Your local nurseryman will usually have a good idea what sort of proteas grow well in your area.

Proteas dislike being shifted so make sure they go in the right place first off. Before setting off to the nursery have a walk around your garden or the area you wish to plant and ask yourself some questions. Where is the drainage best? Are there different soil types? Where is there the most sunlight? What size plants do you need? Does the plant have a special purpose (for example, a windbreak)?

Then make up your list according to the answers. There are now so many protea varieties available that there will be one to suit almost every type of situation. A sketch plan will often help. Show each plant full size and take your plan along with you to the nursery.

Buying Plants

When selecting your protea plants from the nursery look for strong healthy plants. Proteas that look sick at the nursery will usually die after planting. Strong, healthy protea plants should have fresh bushy growth at the stem tips or be showing signs of sending out new growth.

Never buy a plant with any black leaves or 'sooty' material on the leaves and check the lower stem for blackness or signs of rot.

Make sure the plant is not too big for the pot. A few roots growing out the drainage holes frequently indicate a healthy plant, but a pot-bound plant often has a twisted root system and

will usually die or remain stunted. If you are unsure ask the nurseryman to carefully slip it out of the pot to show you the root system.

Also be careful of any plants showing leaves with a blotchy green or yellow appearance as this usually means that they have some sort of nutrient deficiency.

Protea plants can usually be purchased in 75 mm (3"), 150 mm (6") or 200 mm (8") pots. Although the large pots are more expensive they will usually give the best results.

Larger plants will have stronger and hardier root systems and are more visible for mowing and cultivation. However with protea plants the health and vigour of the plant is the most important thing to look for. Select plants that have fresh new growth or new shoots.

One last thing to make sure of is that the plant has been 'hardened off', which means that it has been growing outdoors in close to full sunlight. Proteas love good ventilation and lots of sunlight, but if kept in a shadehouse or similar place and then planted straight into the garden they are often too 'soft' to survive. Plants purchased from air-conditioned supermarkets should be carefully checked.

Where to Grow Proteas

In South Africa proteas grow on decomposed granite soils, which are well drained, acid and low in fertility. They are also generally found in open sunny situations.

You will need to select a site which is open to direct sunlight for all (or most) of the day. Proteas dislike humid conditions and thrive in well ventilated sunny positions. Some of the best sites for proteas are north-facing slopes exposed to the wind.

Proteas like high daytime temperatures up to

35°C but also need to cool down at night. Most species will tolerate quite severe frosts, but heavy frosts will burn off new growth and may even kill young plants.

Soil for proteas must be well drained and friable as they will not tolerate wet feet for long periods. Sandy loams, granite sands or well drained clay-loam soils are suitable. The lighter soils are the best, but good drainage seems to be the most important factor.

Acid soil is a general requirement for most species of protea with a soil pH of between 5.0 and 7.0 being the best. A simple soil test kit can be purchased from most plant nurseries or landcare stores. However, there are some species, such as *Protea obtusifolia*, which will tolerate alkaline soils.

Proteas grow very well in very poor soils and resent addition of fertilisers. Proteas are actively poisoned by higher levels of phosphorus.

Fertilisers generally do not need to be added, however many species will benefit from a small addition of slow-release nitrogen/potassium fertilisers and trace elements after they have been planted for a few years. Animal manures should not be used.

Proteas have the unique ability to absorb nutrients from very poor soils. This is done through special tufts of very fine roots called proteoid roots. These are very delicate and are found generally close to the surface, so surface cultivation should be avoided around proteas or carried out very carefully. Mulching or a shallow-rooted lawn is the best alternative to cultivating close to plants.

If drainage is suspect, especially in very flat areas, raised mounds or beds will be of great benefit by increasing drainage. Many commercial plantations are planted along rows of mounds.

Planting

Correct planting is important for successfully establishing your new protea plants.

Firstly you should thoroughly water the plants in the pots several hours before planting. This is very important as it allows the plant to cope with some dehydration due to the shock of having its roots disturbed during planting.

The hole should be dug much larger and deeper than the pot size and then back-filled to about the depth of the pot. The loosened soil below the roots will allow easier penetration of the new root growth and will also prevent excess water build up inside the new hole.

In very dry soils, especially sandy ones, it may be necessary to fill the hole with water and let it soak away before planting. This decreases the water resistance of very dry soil and allows watering after planting to be totally effective.

Carefully remove the plant from the pot by tipping it upside down and tapping the edge of the pot against a solid surface.

If the roots are coiled try to straighten them out as much as possible. If they are seriously coiled you may need to trim some off, but try to keep major root disturbance to a minimum. Carefully tease out any matted fine brown roots and remove damaged or rotting areas.

Carefully place the plant in the hole with the pot soil about 1 cm below soil level. Carefully back-fill the hole, pressing the soil around the plant firmly but without damaging any of the roots. Do not build soil up around the stem as this may induce a fungal disease called collar rot.

Water in well with at least 4 litres of water to begin with. Another 4 litres about one day later would also be very advantageous. Remember, 90 per cent of young plant deaths are due to dehydration for one reason or another.

Place mulch around the plant if required.

Mulching

Mulching has many advantages for all types of gardening and is especially useful for proteas.

Mulching is highly recommended for four main reasons:
1. Reduces weed growth.
2. Acts as an insulating layer to keep in soil warmth or prevents soil becoming too hot.
3. Traps in soil moisture and reduces the need for watering.
4. Keeps the soil conditioned and also adds nutrients as it decomposes.

Proteas have quite shallow root systems and resent any cultivation close to the plants. Mulching reduces the need for cultivation by attracting worms and other useful organisms which keep the soil friable. It can also prevent or reduce weed growth, greatly reducing the need to cultivate. Many commercial growers use mulches along the rows with grassy swards between to help soak up excess water.

Mulch is best applied at planting but must be kept away from the stem to prevent collar rot from fungal attack. The mulch should be spread at least 5–8 cm thick (or up to 10–15 cm thick for straw and hay).

Woven plastic weed mat is becoming very popular with commercial and home gardens. It is long lasting, easy to lay and allows the soil to breath while also allowing water to penetrate.

Some mulches such as fresh sawdust may cause a problem called nitrogen downturn which is a reduction in the amount of nitrogen available to the plant. This is due to decay organisms using up all the nitrogen while breaking down the mulch. If fresh sawdust is used, slow-release fertiliser may be added to allow for the loss of nitrogen. Well aged sawdust or pinebark is much more suitable. Remember not to use animal manures or stable straw.

Useful types of mulch:

sawdust	pinebark
woodchips	gravel/crushed rock
coarse river sand	straw
grass hay	woven weed mat
newspaper	black plastic sheeting

Watering

Proteas are naturally very hardy and most species do not have a great requirement for water; however, most deaths of young plants are due to water stress.

In their natural habitat of southern Africa proteas are adapted to growing in a huge variety of conditions and so their requirement for water varies greatly. (See species descriptions.) In higher rainfall areas (over 700 mm per year) established protea plants will probably require little supplementary water, but extra watering in the drier months will improve flower stem length, flower quality and plant growth rate.

Trickle irrigation systems are by far the best and most efficient method of watering proteas. This allows the soil to stay moist without wasting

water or increasing humidity around the plant, which may cause fungal diseases. The amount of water will obviously be governed by the local climate and soil type. Care must be taken not to overwater as this may encourage root-damaging fungi.

Young plants should be watered in thoroughly on planting and again at regular intervals in warmer seasons. Regular deep waterings are far better than frequent shallow waterings. It does not hurt protea plants if the soil dries out a little between waterings.

The water used for irrigation should be of good quality. Brackish or alkaline water may badly affect protea plants' growth, as will water with a high salt content. Some dam or lake water may also contain spores of one of the most deadly protea diseases, the cinnamon fungus (*Phytophthora cinnamomi*), especially if it drains from bushland naturally carrying this soil-borne fungus.

Queen protea, mulched with weed mat and watered by drip irrigation

Some hints on watering proteas

1. Select plants which suit your watering capabilities.
2. Use mulches to conserve water.
3. Probe the soil to test water content; it should be moist 2 cm below the surface.
4. Water in the cool period of the day (or at night if you have an automatic watering system).
5. Regular deep waterings are far more effective than frequent shallow irrigation which may encourage shallow root growth.
6. Use a drip system if possible.

7. Take care with hand watering not to wash the soil away from the surface roots especially near the stem.
8. Make a shallow bowl or trench around each plant to retain moisture during the summer.

Fertilisers

Proteas in general will grow in very nutrient-poor soils and have a very small requirement for phosphorus and potassium especially. They are in fact quite actively poisoned by excess phosphorus and low or zero-phosphorus fertilisers should be used. In most areas and most soils proteas will grow very well without any extra nutrients.

Research has shown that recommending a fertiliser for proteas is very risky due to the variable nature of the plants and the variety of soil types. In very poor soils, however, proteas have shown an excellent response in growth rate and flower quality to fertiliser addition. There are several fertilisers worth trying and trial and error for your situation is probably the best method.

Recommended fertilisers for proteas

1. Slow release fertiliser beads
   —NPK (low phosphorus)
   —NK (zero phosphorus)
2. Soluble NPK (low phosphorus) through drip systems
3. Nitrogen (e.g. urea formaldehyde or ammonium sulphate)
4. Potassium chloride (for soils low in potassium)
In some areas the addition of trace elements may improve the growth rate and vigour of proteas. Trace elements are minerals such as iron, magnesium and copper which are required by plants in very small quantities. If the soil is lacking in these the plant may show poor growth or leaf yellowing. They can be purchased as a general soluble trace element mix and are very easy to apply as a foliar spray or liquid fertiliser.

When to fertilise

Fertilising on planting is probably not necessary and if not done correctly may put added stress on the young plant. It is probably best to wait until the plant is well established before trying fertilisers.

As with most plants, fertilisers should be added just before the growth seasons of autumn and spring. The soil should be moist and the fertilisers should be well watered in after adding.

Where to place fertilisers

The fertiliser should be placed evenly around the plant under the dripline of the canopy. It should be kept well away from the main trunk to avoid burning the bark. If cultivation is needed it should be very light to avoid disturbing surface roots. Two or three small applications a year are much more advisable than one large one which may be toxic to the plant.

In general, fertilising may be beneficial for established proteas, but take care.

Staking

If at all possible staking of protea plants should be avoided. Proteas are shallow rooted by nature and if they are staked heavily as young plants will never develop a root system strong enough to support a large plant. An unstaked plant moves about in the wind and develops a stronger trunk and roots.

Young plants should be pruned to promote sturdier growth which will reduce the need for staking.

If staking is absolutely necessary then it should be done with loose, soft strapping. Old stockings, cloth or horticultural tape are the best for this purpose. The plant should be tied loosely to two or three stakes spaced around the trunk (see diagram).

Growing Proteas in Tubs

Many members of the Protea family are suitable for growing in large tubs or half wine barrels. Tubs or pots larger than 40 cm in diameter should be used, and they should have large drainage holes in the bottom to allow the free passage of water. The bottom 5 cm should be filled with broken pots, coarse gravel or road screenings to prevent the drainage holes blocking up.

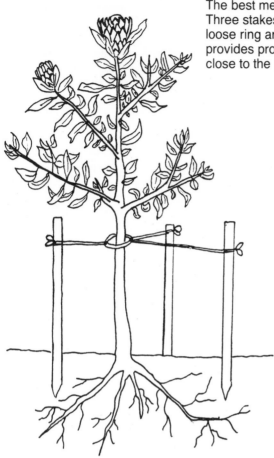

The best method for staking Proteas. Three stakes, evenly spaced, tied to a loose ring around the trunk also provides protection from mowers close to the plant

Pruning

There are several reasons why pruning proteas is very important. Many gardeners and growers end up with ugly, straggly plants due to poor pruning techniques or no pruning at all. These plants will also produce far less blooms than a well pruned protea.

Why should we prune proteas? Pruning

1. Promotes better quality blooms on longer stems.
2. Creates bushier and more compact plants.
3. Reduces susceptibility to disease.
4. Can extend the life of the plant.
5. May alter flowering times.
6. May greatly increase the number of stems or blooms.

Pruning techniques vary slightly for different types of protea but in general there are some basic rules we should follow.

Timing of pruning

Mature plants are pruned by picking flowers. During picking any dead, diseased, damaged or twisted stems should be removed as well. In general it is best to prune proteas just before the start of the main growth seasons of autumn and spring.

Young growing plants can be tip pruned at any time to promote side shoots by simply pinching out the growth shoots.

Pruning tools

A good quality sharp pair of secateurs should be used. Either bypass or anvil-type secateurs are both suitable but they must be very sharp and clean. Blunt or damaged secateurs produce rough cuts which promote fungal attack.

You will probably, at some stage, need a long-handled pair of pruning shears or a small pruning saw for the larger branches.

If several plants are to be pruned, the secateurs or saw should be washed in antiseptic solution between plants to avoid transferring disease from one plant to the next.

A free-draining potting mix should then be added. A mix made up of mostly composted pine bark and coarse sand is the best. If using a commercial mix make sure it does not contain too much fertiliser and especially *no* phosphorus.

The protea should be planted leaving approximately 5 cm of space at the top of the tub to aid watering.

The potted protea should be watered regularly but not over watered. Check the soil moisture 5–6 cm below the surface before watering.

The tub should be placed in a warm sunny spot. Many proteas will tolerate shade for a few hours each day but should be placed so that for most of the day they are in full sun. Proteas grown in tubs should be kept very well pruned to prevent them becoming too large or untidy. Check Chapter 6 for suitable species for growing in tubs.

Thinning out

Thinning out involves the removal of excess branches or shoots. There may be excessive shoot growth, especially along lower stems, which if not removed will reduce the overall flower quality and stem length. This happens commonly on many leucadendrons and leucospermums. When thinning out the plant, cut the stems as close as possible to the main branch. Twisted branches or branches growing towards the ground should also be cut back flush with the main stem.

Heading back

'Heading back' is the term used for cutting back the stem to promote shoot growth. This may be done when the flowers are harvested or when we are carrying out a tidy up pruning. In general, the stem should be cut back to 10 cm from where it has branched off the main stem, and the cut should be made just above a large healthy leaf. If the stem is cut where there are small weak leaves or diseased leaves new shoots may fail to appear and the stem may rot backwards down the plant.

Only strong healthy stems should be headed as these will need to carry the new season's growth. Weak, spindly or damaged stems should be cut off flush with the stem.

Heading should not be overdone. If too much heading is carried out on a plant it may result in too much bushy growth and reduce flower stem length and quality. Heading and thinning need to be balanced for the best flower production.

Pruning to alter flowering

Pruning can be used to manipulate the timing of flowering or the number and size of flowers on a plant.

New shoots which appear after pruning will form the flower stems for the next season. Most proteas, leucadendrons and leucospermums take 12 months from shooting to grow and produce a flower. In some of the *Protea* species and hybrids (*P. cynaroides*, *P.* 'Pink Ice', *P. magnifica*, *P. speciosa*, *P. grandiceps*) the cycle from shoot growth to flowering is much longer and it can take up to two years for a flower to form on the new stem.

To show how pruning can be used to alter flowering time we will take as an example the management of *Leucadendron* 'Silvan Red'. Given several rows of this cultivar, the grower

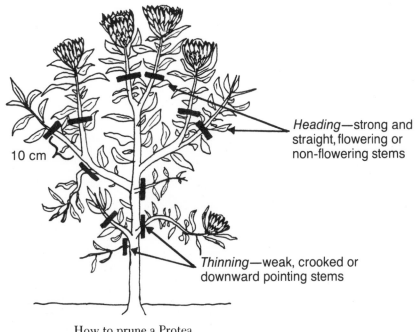

10 cm

Heading—strong and straight, flowering or non-flowering stems

Thinning—weak, crooked or downward pointing stems

How to prune a Protea

could prune the first row in, say, August; these plants would then have flowers in approximately 12 months time, i.e. August the next year. The grower could then prune a row each fortnight to three weeks and so have a continuous supply of mature flowers the year after. This method works reasonably well with most proteas and leucadendrons but of course is very dependent on seasonal conditions and how specific each species' flowering season is.

Pruning can also be used to alter the bush shape and number of flowers. Home gardeners may wish to have a bushier protea plant with many blooms. This can be achieved by heading back as many stems as possible and reducing thinning. This will produce a higher number of shorter-stemmed, smaller blooms.

Cut flower growers who require longer stem length and larger quality blooms will thin plants more heavily, heading only the strongest, straightest stems.

Pruning young protea plants

Pruning techniques vary slightly according to the type of protea. Proteas can be split into four useful pruning groupings.

1. Most *Protea* species and larger-flowered *Leucadendron* species

Many home gardeners are afraid to prune their young proteas after planting. This often leads to long straggly stems and an ugly plant which will never produce many flowers.

As soon as the young plant has a shoot or main stem longer than 30 cm it should be tip pruned. This can be done simply by pinching out the growing bud or by cutting off about 2.5 cm with a pair of secateurs. This rule also applies to proteas in their second season. You should also

Tip prune

Cut back to 2 or 3 main straight stems

Cut back each stem to 10 cm from the branch

A few months after planting · 12 months later · After two years

Where to prune Proteas in the first three years

Protea compacta showing tall untidy growth habit due to lack of pruning in the first few years

Tip pruning a young *Protea* 'Pink Ice'

thin any weak or spindly growth leaving three to four main stems.

In the third season the protea can be allowed to flower. After flowering the stems can be cut back to 10 cm from the main stem branch. Any side growth, spindly branches or branches growing towards the ground should be pruned off flush with the stem.

2. Proteas with lignotubers (e.g. *Protea cynaroides*)

Some protea species have a large swelling of the trunk just under or at the soil surface called a lignotuber. This acts as an underground trunk and in nature is an adaptation to surviving fire or severe damage. The lignotuber bears dormant buds which shoot after fire or major foliage loss.

This group of proteas includes *Protea cynaroides* (king protea) and *Leucadendron salignum* and its many hybrids (such as 'Safari Sunset' or 'Silvan Red'). The leucadendrons are usually pruned in the conventional manner.

Protea cynaroides can be pruned in two ways. It can be carefully pruned to create a shrub-like habit by pruning in the normal fashion. This, however, is quite difficult and often results in a very spreading and messy plant.

Most commercial growers prefer to prune the stems almost back to ground level leaving about 5–7 cm of stem. New shoots will appear from the lignotuber and in 12–18 months will produce a flower bud.

Many home gardeners have found *Protea cynaroides* reluctant to flower. The best way to induce flowering is to cut all the stems back to 5–7 cm from the ground. The new shoots will usually produce flowers.

3. Young leucospermums

Young leucospermum plants should also be tip pruned to encourage a bushier, more compact habit for the first six months to a year after planting. They can then be allowed to flower and the flower stems cut back to 10 cm from the main branch.

With leucospermums it is usually quite important to thin out most of the weaker flowering stems or shoots which have failed to flower. This will induce larger flower heads on much longer stems in the next flowering season. Leucospermums often have the tendency to produce masses of short-stemmed flowers and non-flowering shoots if they are only headed back with little thinning out. Of course this form may be desirable to some home gardeners who wish to have a dense, showy shrub.

In very rich soils some species of leucospermum will also produce masses of side shoots which need to be thinned out.

Disbudding leucospermums

Many species of leucospermum will produce more than one bud on a flowering stem. This will often produce one good quality flower and one or more poor quality blooms. In the home garden this may not matter but if larger, high quality bloom is required the sideways pointing buds or weaker buds should be gently broken off by hand.

Flowering time can also be altered if required by breaking off the larger buds on some stems. The smaller buds will then develop later on. In this way a grower can spread the flowering time of the leucospermum over 2–3 months rather than having it concentrated in a shorter period.

First year
Where to cut
to form a shrub

After 12 months

For longer stems
cut back to ground level

How to prune *Protea cynaroides*

Leucospermum stem with multiple flower buds

Leucospermum after disbudding. Note only one strong flower bud has been left

4. Large multiflowering leucadendrons

Leucadendron species in this group include:

L. salicifolium	*L. eucalyptifolium*
L. coniferum	*L. xanthaconus*
L. conicum	*L. uliginosum*
L. macowanii	*L. meridianum*

This group of leucadendrons tends to grow very quickly and branch profusely.

In the first year of growth tip pruning can be carried out all over the plant.

In subsequent years the branches should be cut back to approximately 10 cm from the main branch after flowering has finished or during flower harvesting.

If plants in this group are to be used for harvesting cut flowers they will need to be cut back generously each year. Most of these leucadendron species will grow to over 4 metres if let go, so if they are not cut back severely a ladder will be required to harvest the best stems which are usually near the top of the plant.

Maintenance pruning

After the initial two to three years most pruning can be carried out by picking flower stems or cutting off old blooms after flowering has finished.

At this time any weak or damaged stems should also be removed and any thinning out carried out; stems growing downwards or along the ground should be cut off flush with the main stem.

Many of the larger-flowered leucadendrons, such as *L.* 'Safari Sunset', *L. laureolum* and *L.* 'Silvan Red', may benefit from fairly severe thinning out procedures. With these types of leucadendron all old flower stems or non-flowering shoots should be cut back to 10 cm from the branch. Then all weak shoots or stems should be removed leaving only three to four strong healthy stems at the end of each branch. These will then produce long, straight, healthy flowering stems in 12 months from pruning. Also any soft, downy growth along the lower branches should be removed.

Restricting the number of flowers on all protea, leucadendron and leucospermum plants will always produce better quality blooms on longer stems. How many stems to thin out and remove will always be the choice of the grower depending on what is required of the plant.

3 Propagation

Most proteas are fairly easy to propagate by either seed or cuttings if a few simple rules are followed.

Propagation can be divided into sexual propagation (from seed) and asexual or vegetative propagation (from cuttings or grafting).

Some species are quite easy to grow from seed, however many protea species are very difficult and have 'dormancy' systems which make them very difficult to germinate. Also propagation by seed is no guarantee of gaining a plant like the parent. Proteas cross-pollinate easily within the species providing variation. They also cross-pollinate readily between species to produce hybrids.

Propagation by cuttings at least guarantees that the new plant will be genetically identical to the parent plant.

Despite proteas having a reputation for being difficult to propagate there is no reason why any enthusiast or grower should not be able to propagate most of the common species.

Propagating Equipment and Structures

The range of suitable propagating structures is restricted only by the individual's budget and the scale on which he wishes to propagate.

Protea cuttings and seed will both grow to their best advantage in hothouse or greenhouse conditions with a regularly maintained water supply. The home gardener may provide these with simple homemade structures or even something as simple as a large pot or box covered with plastic.

To start with everyone will require a clean sharp pair of secateurs, a sharp razor or suitable knife and a range of pots and seedling trays.

Either anvil-type or bypass secateurs are suitable. The anvil type is much easier to sharpen properly, but often tends to damage the stems being cut. Sharp bypass secateurs give a much cleaner cut.

There are many methods of providing the warmth and humidity required for cutting or seed growth. A few of the most popular propagating structures are outlined below.

A box covered in plastic

To make a mini greenhouse simply cover a suitable box with a sheet of clear plastic secured around the box with string. Waxed cardboard boxes, wooden boxes and polystyrene foam fruit boxes are all suitable.

The bottom of the box can be filled with sand in which the pots can be half buried. The sand not only traps extra moisture but also acts as an insulator. The advantage of these box greenhouses is that they can be easily placed in a warm area in cold weather or under shady trees in hot sunny weather. Alternatively a piece of shadecloth can be thrown over them on hot sunny days.

Pots covered with a plastic bag

This works in the same way as the box method but on a smaller scale.

Simply fill a pot with the cutting or seed mix and plant your seeds or treated cuttings. Then bend two pieces of wire into a U shape and press them point down at right angles to each other in the pot. Then cover with a plastic shopping bag or clear plastic food bag.

The disadvantage of this method and the box method is that sometimes the humidity is too great and the seedlings or cuttings may rot. To prevent this happening it is best not to overwater these structures but just keep the cutting mix slightly damp.

Heated propagating boxes or frames

There are many types of smaller propagating boxes or frames. Most of these have some sort of heating element enclosed in the bottom to warm the cuttings which aids rooting. These types of unit are excellent for some of the more difficult to strike *Protea* species.

They can be filled with cutting mix and then the cuttings planted directly into the mix. A better method is to bury small plastic cutting tubes into the mix and then plant the cuttings in these using the standard method.

Some of the larger, more expensive units have their own misting system, but most have to be hand watered regularly.

The major advantage of these units is that cuttings may be struck in the colder months of the year when this would usually be very difficult.

With these units great care must be taken to keep all materials very clean as fungus attack is very common due to the warm, moist conditions. To avoid fungal diseases care should be taken not to overwater the cutting mix. A good drenching with a general fungicide like Benlate after putting the cuttings in, and again one week later, is also advisable.

Glasshouses

These come in a large range of sizes and shapes from small backyard units to large commercial structures. They can be covered in glass, fibreglass, rigid plastic or perspex. Glasshouses can be heated using electric floor heating, gas or even wood, but with proteas this is mostly unnecessary.

Glasshouses are excellent for striking protea cuttings or raising seedlings but are in general quite expensive. In recent years, however, many small kit form glasshouses have come on the market at very reasonable prices especially those covered in fibreglass sheeting or rigid plastic instead of glass.

Polythene igloos

These structures are both very successful and very inexpensive. They usually consist of an aluminium or galvanised tubular frame covered with a polythene film. Some very tough shrink-resistant and UV-resistant films have been produced in recent years with a life of up to five years in suitable conditions.

The lower edges of the poly cover can be either buried, to hold them down, or attached to a wooden frame. Some igloos have sides that can be raised at the bottom to allow extra ventilation in hot weather. In the warmer seasons poly igloos can be whitewashed to reduce radiation or covered with shadecloth, an easier and more effective method which has the advantage of being easy to remove when required.

The floor of the poly igloo can be covered with either road metal screenings or woven weedmat. Both these materials allow easy drainage of excess water.

Polythene igloos come in all sizes and can easily be extended just by adding more hoops.

Propagating Proteas from Cuttings

Propagation from cuttings is by far the easiest and most practical method of vegetative

A small electric propagating box used for striking cuttings or germinating seeds

Polythene igloo with a shadecloth cover to reduce summer heat

propagation for protea plants. Grafting, budding and tissue culture have all been used but are not really practical for the home gardener. Most protea species will strike readily if a few simple rules are followed.

The main advantages of growing proteas from cuttings are:

1. You are guaranteed that the offspring will be genetically identical to the parent plant and display identical form, leaf and flower characteristics if grown under similar conditions.
2. Proteas grown from cuttings will flower much earlier than seed-grown proteas, often in the first year if they are left unpruned.
3. Cutting-grown plants will tend to be lower growing and more compact.
4. Young plants have proven to be sturdier and are less likely to die from fungal attack than seed-grown proteas.
5. Many hybrid proteas (e.g. *Protea* 'Pink Ice') are sterile and cannot produce viable seed. These can only be propagated by cuttings.

When to take cuttings

For greatest success, cuttings should be taken from semi-hardened plant material. Generally this is the new growth from the last growth season (either autumn or spring) which has hardened off for a few months. Taking the correct cutting material is probably the most important aspect of obtaining a high strike rate with your cuttings.

During spring lush shoot growth usually develops. This then hardens off over summer and is usually ready for cuttings in late summer or early autumn. The readiness of the cutting material will vary considerably with seasonal conditions and judging when it is 'ripe' is really a matter for trial and error.

Most *Protea* and *Leucospermum* species are carrying semi-hardened cutting material from early autumn and it should be taken before the cooler winter months. The *Leucadendron* species in general are easier to propagate and cuttings may be taken from late summer to mid winter.

It should be noted however that cuttings taken later in autumn and winter may have a lower strike rate due to the cooler climatic conditions and shorter days during the time they are forming roots.

Taking a side-shoot cutting from *Protea* 'Pink Ice'

Cutting preparation

Protea species

With most *Protea* species great care should be taken to select the correct type of growth for cuttings.

The most successful cuttings by far are the semi-hardwood side shoots which come from just below a forming bud or flower. If these side shoots are allowed to harden off they have proved to have an excellent strike rate. Stem cuttings or cuttings from shoot growth lower on the stem will also strike but will have a lower success rate and be much slower to strike.

Leucadendrons and leucospermums

Cuttings from *Leucadendron* and *Leucospermum* species are in general easier to strike than those from *Protea* species. Cuttings can be taken from the plants over a longer period of time as long as the cutting material is not too soft; most semi-hardwood growth should strike.

Either tip or stem cuttings may be taken, but material closer to the tip usually proves easier to strike. Cutting material from lower down the stem often proves to be too woody and is difficult and slow to strike.

General rules for taking cuttings

These simple rules should be followed for successful propagation using cuttings:

1. Cuttings should be taken early in the morning when it is cool and moist. The cutting material will be fully hydrated and will have a much greater chance of survival.

2. Cuttings should be placed in a plastic bag and sprayed with water. They should only be kept for a few hours before treatment and planting, in a cool place away from direct sunlight.

3. Cuttings should be 15–25 cm long if possible. Smaller cuttings will strike but larger cuttings have a far greater chance of survival. Cuttings should also be from the *thickest* shoots; thin stems are far more susceptible to fungal attack and dehydration.

4. The leaves on the bottom half to two-thirds of the cutting should be carefully removed, without tearing the outer bark (cambium) layer of the stem, by pulling them towards the tip of the cutting. Removing the leaves reduces the amount of water lost by the cutting through transpiration. Removal of too many leaves will reduce the strike rate as it is believed that materials from the leaves actually induce root formation.

   Some protea and leucadendron species have quite delicate stems and with these species the leaves may need to be cut off with a sharp razor to avoid damaging the cambium layer.

   With some large-leafed protea species it may be necessary to trim the leaves back by one-third to half; however, this may make the cutting more susceptible to fungal attack and should be avoided if possible.

5. The cuttings should be planted in the cutting mix to about one-third of their total length and pressed in firmly. A cutting which is loose in the mixture will rarely strike.

6. The cuttings should be gently but thoroughly watered in and given a thorough drenching with a general purpose fungicide such as Captan or Benlate.

7. The cuttings should be kept moist but not too wet. A humid atmosphere around the leaf part of the cutting seems to be very important. If the cutting survives the first four to five weeks it will generally strike.

Hormone treatment

Treating protea cuttings with a plant hormone (or auxin) will greatly increase the percentage strike rate and the strength of the roots formed. By far the most successful hormone treatment used is indole butyric acid (IBA) which is widely available in nurseries and from horticultural material suppliers. It comes both in powder form and as a liquid mix which is usually diluted with water before use. If you are mixing the hormone yourself from the crystalline form it is best used at a concentration of 4000 ppm. Most commercial preparations come in this concentration.

Powders give satisfactory results but it is often easy to apply too much, resulting in burnt and damaged plant tissue. This happens especially with those species with hairy stems.

The cutting should be moistened and the bottom 1–2 cm dipped in the powder; the excess is removed by tapping the cutting. Left-over powder should be discarded as it may be contaminated.

Liquid IBA has proven to be the most effective and efficient hormone treatment for proteas. It is difficult to 'overtreat' cuttings and many cuttings can be processed at once. It should be

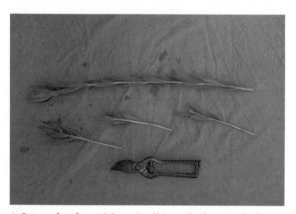

A *Leucadendron* 'Silvan Red' stem before and after processing to produce two stem cuttings and a tip cutting

A *Protea* 'Pink Ice' stem with ideal side-shoots for cuttings and two processed cuttings

Cuttings being dipped in a liquid indole butyric acid mix to promote root growth

noted however that IBA breaks down in direct sunlight and high temperatures. It should be stored out of the light in a refrigerator and should be used within three months of mixing for best results. Make sure when purchasing root-promoting liquids from nurseries that they are fresh.

The cuttings should be dipped to a depth of approximately 1–2 cm for 10 seconds. If the cuttings are left in the hormone for too long tissue damage will occur, resulting in cutting death.

Cutting mix

The most successful cutting mix for protea cuttings is a mixture of two parts coarse washed river sand to one part good quality peat moss. If watering may be a problem up to one part sand to one part peat moss may be used to increase water retention. This of course also increases the chance of fungal attack.

Fine ground polystyrene foam can be used as a replacement for the sand in the same proportion with equal success.

If an efficient watering system is available a mixture of three parts sand to one part peat moss will also give excellent results and reduces the chance of cutting death due to rotting.

It is important to use a good quality, sterilised peat moss. Most commercial peat comes pre-sterilised in plastic bags or bales. The sand should be washed to remove any soils or contaminants and sharp coarse sand gives the best results.

Containers

Protea cuttings should be placed in separate containers for the best results. They can be placed in groups in large pots but if one cutting becomes contaminated then they usually all die.

Protea cuttings seem to strike more readily in individual tubes. Small black plastic tubes approximately 35 mm in diameter and 75 mm high give the best results. Larger tubes may be used for larger-diameter cuttings such as those of *P. cynaroides* but they usually take longer to form roots in the larger tubes.

Plastic trays with separate small compartments are gaining popularity with the nursery trade and require far less handling time than individual tubes.

Conditions for striking cuttings

Protea cuttings will strike most readily when kept in a warm moist atmosphere. It is important not to overheat the cuttings as this will cause leaf blackening and death quite rapidly. It is also important not to overwater them as this promotes rotting of the stems. It has also been found that if the cutting medium is kept just slightly moist the cuttings will root more readily. If the cutting medium is kept very wet the cuttings may tend to over callus and not strike, or may take much longer to strike.

If the cuttings are housed in a small hot house or igloo a mist watering system is the best. This keeps the environment cool and moist without over-wetting the mixture.

Hand watering is also quite suitable. However, as watering may need to be done two to three times a day in warmer weather it may be a large task. A very fine spray should be used to avoid moving or loosening the cuttings.

Cuttings should be well spaced to allow adequate ventilation between them and equal exposure to light.

If heat beds, which give bottom heat, are a viable proposition these may be useful for some protea species. However, some species, especially *Protea repens*, resent too much heat which causes leaf blackening and death. In areas with a very cold winter bottom heat may be necessary to gain a higher strike rate, but most protea cuttings will strike eventually without any heat from artificial sources.

The best temperature for striking protea cuttings is 20–27°C in the day and above 12°C at night. If the daytime temperature is exceeding the maximum frequently, shading with shade-cloth may be necessary.

Transplanting cuttings

After approximately 10 weeks most of the cuttings should be beginning to send out roots. Some leucadendron and leucospermum species may take as little as 5 weeks to strike whereas some protea species may take up to 12 months to send out roots.

If the cuttings have been placed in individual pots it is simply a matter of gently tapping out the cutting and soil together from the pot to check whether roots have formed. Great care is needed as these first roots are very easily broken or damaged.

A leucospermum cutting showing excellent root formation

If the cuttings have developed a strong network of roots then they are ready for potting up or planting.

If you are planting your struck cuttings straight from the cutting tube you should harden them off outside the propagating structure for at least two weeks before planting.

Potting up

It is usually best to pot up your fully struck protea cuttings before planting so they can achieve a more viable size.

The cutting and mix should be gently removed from the tube or container by gently tapping it upside down on a hard surface. The cutting should then be planted slightly below its previous soil surface and pressed in firmly.

A very free-draining potting mix should be used. The mix should also be free of too much added fertiliser. Some of the soil-less mixtures using mainly composted pine bark and coarse sand are the best for proteas. Some commercial nurseries also add a small percentage of crushed polystyrene or polystyrene beads to open the mixture even further.

A teaspoon of zero-phosphorus, slow-release fertiliser beads should also be added to each pot.

Many commercial nurseries drench the freshly potted cuttings with a broad-spectrum fungicide such as Benlate or Octave to help prevent fungal attack while they are becoming established in the pot.

After potting on the plants can either be placed back into the propagating frame if the weather conditions are cool or put outside in a shadehouse or some other suitably protected site. The new plants will need to be regularly watered while they become established.

Propagating Proteas from Seed

Growing proteas from seed is both an interesting and rewarding method of propagation.

The main advantage of growing proteas from seed is that because of the natural variation among seed-grown plants and the fact that many species will very readily hybridise, the grower never really knows what sort of plant he will end up with.

Growing plants from seed can also be cheaper and easier for many gardeners than propagation by cuttings.

Obtaining seed

Protea seeds can be readily obtained from any of the major seed supply companies. These usually advertise frequently in gardening and horticultural magazines. Some protea seeds, however, are quite expensive and may prove too costly for the home gardener.

Most of the protea family set seeds quite readily, especially the leucadendrons, so harvesting your own seeds is often the best option.

With most of the protea and leucadendron species it is best to pick the flower heads between five and nine months after flowering. If they are picked too early the seeds are not yet ripe and mature, but if picked too late they have often been emptied by insects or the seeds have deteriorated due to moisture and fungal attack.

Protea seeds are usually about the size and shape of an oat seed but are often quite hairy. Viable seeds are plump and firm when squeezed between the fingernails. Seeds should be removed from the dried flower heads and stored in a cool, dry place either in sealed jars or brown paper bags.

Protea seeds have proved to be unreliable in germination rate when stored over long periods and should be planted as soon as possible after harvesting for best results.

With leucadendron species the female cones should be picked after approximately six months. In many species of leucadendron the cones will split open and release their seeds; however some varieties retain their seeds. After gathering the mature cones it is only a matter of placing them in plain paper bags in a warm dry place where the seed follicle will open within weeks to release the seeds. A warm oven may be used to speed up this process. Leucadendron seeds should be stored in a cool dry place and may be stored for long periods of time and retain an excellent germination rate.

Sowing protea seeds

Both autumn and spring are good times to sow your protea seeds although it seems that autumn gives the best results. Another advantage of planting seed in autumn is that the young plants will have a chance to grow to a reasonable size before summer.

Seed dormancy is a problem with many of the protea species and without some form of pre-sowing treatment germination rates may be very poor.

The process of breaking the outer seed coat is known as scarification. This can be achieved by rubbing each seed gently on some fine sandpaper or by scratching the seed with a razor. This is, however, time consuming and can often damage the seed. A better method is to soak the seed for 5–10 minutes in concentratred sulphuric acid. This acid is the same as in standard car batteries and can be obtained from garages.

After soaking in the acid the seed should be washed thoroughly in clean water.

Another method that has found popularity and which has proved very effective with leucospermum seeds is to use hydrogen peroxide in about a one per cent solution. The seeds should be soaked for 24–48 hours.

The mix for sowing protea seeds must be free draining and should be as free as possible from fungal spores. For this reason it is best to use a mixture of three parts coarse washed river sand to one part of fine peat moss. The peat moss can be replaced with spagnum moss or perlite if desired. It is advisable not to use any soil in the seed mix as this will often carry a high level of decay organisms.

The best types of container are either small plastic vegetable seedling punnets or, on a larger scale, plastic seedling trays about 400 × 300 mm. Foam fruit boxes with the tops trimmed down are also suitable.

The container should be filled almost to the top and the mixture pressed down evenly all over.

The seeds should be placed evenly and well spaced all over the tray to allow them to be easily pricked out after germination. If seeds are planted too close together it leads to weak spindly seedlings.

The seeds should be only thinly covered to a depth of about two to three times the width of the seed (approximately 5 mm for most species). The mixture should then be gently pressed down again using a small flat board.

It is advisable, after the initial watering, to drench the mixture with a general fungicide to ensure that any germinating fungal spores are eliminated immediately.

The seed container should now be placed in the propagating structure or in a warm sheltered place. Warmth, either from the propagating structure or produced by artificial means, will greatly speed up germination rates. One easy method for the home gardener is to place a light bulb over the mixture to keep it warm.

The seed mixture should never be allowed to dry out. An automatic mist system, if available, is the best. Otherwise the mixture must be watered regularly using a fine spray.

The seeds will generally germinate in three to six weeks; however, some species such as *Leucadendron argenteum* may take much longer (up to 12 months).

Pricking out protea seedlings

Seedlings should be pricked out of the seed-raising mix as soon as possible after they have developed their first two true leaves and have reached a height of about 2–3 cm.

They should be potted on into containers no larger than about 10 cm in diameter. Both small pots and tubes are suitable.

A dibber or small stick should be used to make a deep hole in the potting mix. The soil around the seedlings should be loosened gently with a knife or something similar and the seedling gently pulled free between the thumb and forefinger.

The roots should be allowed to fall naturally into the hole in the potting mix with no curling or folding. The mixture can then be gently and firmly pressed around the seedling. If the seedling has a large root system it may be necessary to position it over the empty pot and then carefully fill the pot around it, then press the mixture in firmly.

It is often a good idea to water the seedlings with a root-promoting hormone after transplanting, to encourage root growth.

The newly potted plants should now be placed in a shadehouse or propagating frame until they are established and watered regularly.

After two to three weeks some slow-release (zero-phosphorus) fertiliser may be added to the pots. Never plant seedlings into a rich medium as this may cause serious set backs to their growth rate. After they have reached a height of 50–60 mm they may be potted on to a richer potting mix.

Weed growth in the pots should be kept to a minimum especially while the seedlings are growing. A soil sterilising powder may be added to the surface of the pots if weeds are a serious problem. Alternatively a handful of fine gravel or coarse sand can be added to the top of the pot to act as a mulch. If slugs, snails or slaters are present some baits should be placed near the seedling pots as these pests are often fond of young protea plants.

Grafting Proteas

Grafting is usually used when growers have difficulty growing a desired protea due to climatic conditions or persistant disease. Many proteas can be grafted onto hardy rootstock to produce strong viable plants.

Grafting is particularly useful to combat the most serious disease of proteas, *Phytophthora* (cinnamon fungus), which causes root rot. Some of the more susceptible leucospermums can be grafted onto *Phytophthora*-resistant rootstock such as *Protea compacta*, *P. repens*, some of the hybrids such as *P.* 'Pink Ice' or some of the hybrid leucospermums.

Grafting is carried out by the standard methods used for other plants like fruit trees. However it is often necessary to apply regular doses of a general fungicide to the grafted plants until the graft heals.

The best time for grafting proteas is in the spring while autumn grafting also yields excellent results.

4 Pests and Diseases

Proteas in general are quite hardy and disease-resistant plants. Like most plants grown out of their natural environment, proteas tend to become diseased when grown in sites which do not really suit them. They generally require very good drainage and ventilation and often have disease problems in wetter more humid conditions.

With proteas, prevention of disease is often much easier to achieve than a cure. The more serious diseases of proteas are often difficult and very expensive to treat.

In general, to prevent most diseases of your protea plants a few simple rules need to be followed:

1. Choose a healthy vigorous plant from the nursery *completely* free of any dead or spotted leaves. Also check the stem for collar rot.
2. Choose disease-resistant species or strains.
3. Select your site carefully—full sun, plenty of ventilation and good drainage. Improve the drainage if necessary by using a raised bed or a drainage system.
4. Check the soil for acidity or alkalinity.
5. Do not use any animal manures or plant in areas previously heavily fertilised.
6. Keep the plants pruned, especially clear around the lower 20 cm of the trunk. Thin out the centre of denser shrubs to allow for ventilation. Remove immediately damaged or diseased stems.
7. Make sure you wash gloves, secateurs and tools with disinfectant after use and between shrubs.

Treatment of diseases in proteas is quite unreliable. Magic cures for most of the common diseases are not available although some very useful chemicals have become available in recent years.

To aid in the control of the most common diseases the following may be of some assistance.

Soil and Nutrient Disorders

Phosphorus poisoning

Phosphorus poisoning is probably one of the most common nutrient disorders which affects protea plants. It usually results in the death of young shoots, leaf drop, browning of the leaves and eventually plant death. Treatment is almost impossible, prevention being the only real answer. Do not use any fertilisers containing phosphorus, fowl manures or fresh animal manures on protea plants. Do not plant proteas in areas which have been previously heavily fertilised.

Mineral deficiency

Iron deficiency is also a common problem resulting in a distinct loss of colour from the leaves or leaf yellowing. Leaves rich in iron are a fresh bright green colour. Treatment is quite easy using a foliar spray or liquid fertilising with iron chelate or iron sulphate.

Lack of other trace elements, such as potassium, magnesium or zinc, may also result in leaf yellowing or stunted growth. A general soluble trace element mixture should be used to overcome these problems. It can be used as a foliar spray or liquid fertiliser.

Stem Diseases

Collar rot

Collar rot is a common stem disease of protea plants which is easily prevented. It usually occurs when mulches or fresh soil are heaped up around the base of the main stem, allowing fungi to attack the outer layers of the stem. It often results in death, especially of young plants, and at the least will retard growth or cause some leaf death.

To prevent collar rot make sure new plants are planted close to the soil level of the pot and keep mulches at least 5–10 cm from the stem. Improved drainage will also help prevent collar rot. On larger plants the rotten bark should be trimmed away and the area painted with a general fungicide or bordeaux paste.

Sooty mould

Sooty mould is often found on densely growing protea shrubs. This is the result of fungus growing on the sugary secretions of a sucking insect called scale. It is easy to recognise as the branches are covered with a layer of thick sooty powder. Treatment is by spraying with an insecticide such as Maldison or white oil to get rid of the scale. The fungus will disappear over the next few weeks.

Stem cankers

Stem cankers appear as areas of dead or rotting bark which are usually mouldy grey, or sunken and brown. These are usually the result of stem damage by animals or machinery or from branches being broken off. Severe cankers will often cause the weakened stem to break in the wind.

Treatment of stem canker is difficult. If possible damaged branches should be removed, otherwise spraying with Rovral or Benlate may clear up the problem.

Scab disease

Scab disease (Elsinoe disease, corky bark disease) causes raised corky lesions on the stems of leucospermums and leucadendrons. Usually it affects the current season's growth and causes the branches to be distorted and twisted.

Affected areas should all be removed and the plant and neighbouring plants should be treated with a fungicide. Octave seems to be quite effective in preventing new infections.

Fungal Leaf Diseases

Leaf spots

Fungal leaf diseases can vary from a few brown and red spots on the leaves to serious plant-threatening diseases. These are often found on the broad-leaf varieties such as *Protea cynaroides* and *P. grandiceps* and they seriously reduce the commercial value of the blooms, making them worthless for the export market. To prevent leaf spot a regular spraying program with a copper-based spray or a broad-spectrum fungicide like Benlate is required.

Grey mould

Grey mould or *Botrytis* blight is often found in dense proteas growing in sheltered or humid positions. It is caused by a fungus called *Botrytis cinerea* and may cause disfigured flowers and massive leaf death, usually of the new growth. The powdery grey mould is often visible to the naked eye. Treatment is by spraying regularly with Rovral or Captan.

Leaf dieback

Leaf blackening or shoot dieback is a serious disease of proteas caused by a fungus called *Colletotrichum*. The new shoots die back from the tip, and often causing the branch to become black and twisted. Treatment is difficult, however spraying with Octave will help prevent attack by *Colletotrichum*. Great care with disinfecting secateurs will help prevent spread from shrub to shrub.

Drechslera blight

Drechslera blight has caused massive damage of leucospermums in commercial plantations. It causes brown or red lesions on the leaves or rapid dieback of the new shoots or flowers. Most of the more recent leucospermum cultivars have been developed from Drechslera-resistant stock plants.

Treatment is by spraying with Rovral or any benzimidazole fungicide regularly every 2–3 weeks (depending on rainfall).

Root Rot

This is the most serious and costly of all the protea diseases. The major cause of root rot is *Phytophthora cinnamomi* or cinnamon fungus, a naturally occuring fungus which also affects many non-proteaceous plant species.

Cinnamon fungus can be introduced in infected pots or soil. It is also transferred in surface and soil water. It reproduces rapidly in warm wet weather but may be quite dormant during drier times of the year.

Improving soil drainage through raised beds or subsoil drainage systems is an excellent way to reduce the effects of this fungus. It is also important to select the more resistant species or cultivars and sterilise any soil or organic materials coming onto your property.

The most common symptoms of cinnamon fungus are leaf death or shoot die-back. Plants may also become stunted or show poor leaf colour. These symptoms are due to the damaged root system being inadequate to take in the necessary water and mineral ions required by the plant. The disease may also result in the very sudden death of a seemingly healthy adult plant, typically after a long dry spell. This is due to an inadequate root system, and when the plant is pulled up the stunted and distorted roots will usually be quite obvious.

Prevention is certainly the best way to cope with cinnamon fungus, as once it is present it is almost impossible, and is certainly very costly, to eradicate. The soil surrounding the plant can be drenched with fungicide which, at best, will only prevent the disease from occurring for a short period of time.

Many fungicides have been shown to kill the cinnamon fungus in laboratory experiments but have been quite ineffective in the field. Fungicides which have proved quite useful include Fongarid and Ridomil; however there are several experimental fungicides which may be on the market in the near future.

Pests

In general protea plants are rarely killed by animal pests although significant loss of quality may be caused through damage of otherwise A-grade blooms. Unless a particularly serious problem occurs the home gardener rarely needs to worry about pests.

Scale insects

Scale insects are sap-suckers which will grow in colonies along the lower stems of the plant. They may cause death or wilting of the branch by reducing the sap flow. They appear as shiny white scale-like shells attached firmly to the stem.

Scale insects also produce a surgary exudate which often becomes infected with sooty mould. They should be sprayed with Maldison or white oil.

Leaf-chewing caterpillars

Many different kinds of caterpillar may chew the new growth of proteas, especially the *Leucadendron* species. This has been a particular problem with *L.* 'Safari Sunset' and *L.* 'Silvan Red' grown specifically for export. The chewed leaves or bracts make the blooms worthless for sale. Identification is easy from the chewed or rough leaf margins or leaves rolled up to make cocoons.

Treatment is by a regular spraying program with a general insecticide like pyrethrum or Maldison.

Mites

Mites often cause minor leaf damage in commercial and home garden plantations. They are members of the arachnid group of animals (e.g. spiders) and are not insects. They feed by sucking sap, especially from the leaves. Mite damage can be identified by the light green or yellow mottled appearance of the leaves. The leaves may also take on a silvery, dry appearance. Treatment is relatively easy with a spraying program and several very effective miticide sprays are available.

Nematode root disease

Nematodes (members of the worm family) may cause root damage in proteas resulting in stunted growth, or sudden death when the plant is subjected to water stress. A group of soil nematodes belonging to the genus *Melodogyne* causes a disease called root knot. The nematodes live inside the infected roots causing large knots or galls to form which disrupt the normal function of the roots. Nematode infection may occur in a variety of ways. Infected potting soil, soil, water and new plants have all been shown to carry the nematodes or their eggs.

Effective treatment of nematodes, as with other soil-related diseases, is very difficult. Prevention through improved soil drainage and a high level of sanitation is important. Sterilising potting soils is very important and treatment of new plants while they are still in their pots is recommended. Methyl bromide fumigation has proved effective but is difficult and expensive. Planting resistant species or selected resistant varieties is probably the best protection in areas where these nematodes may cause a serious problem.

Other animal pests

Cats, possums, rabbits, hares, kangaroos and some birds may all cause problems at different times, especially when their usual food source is in short supply.

Good plantation fencing or individual tree guards are the best protection possible, especially while the plants are young. Wrapping the trunks of large plants with aluminium foil, bituminous paper or tin may also prevent climbing or clawing animals from damaging the trunks.

There are repellant sprays available which have proved effective against possums, rabbits and hares. Garlic sprays will also repel some animal pests.

Some parrot species may chew young buds, especially on new young plants. Tree guards will help prevent this.

Nectar-feeding birds and bees will quickly damage open protea flowers and they should be picked as soon as the bud is ready to open to prevent this.

5 Proteas for Pleasure and Profit

Proteas have certainly become extremely popular commercial and garden plants since the early 1980s—not only because they make outstanding garden specimens but also because of their usefulness as a long-lasting cut flower. A small plantation of mixed proteas will supply a keen floral artist with plenty of material and may also provide extra income through cut flower sales.

The Cut Flower Market

The cut flower industry is extremely diverse in nature. It varies from the home gardener selling a few proteas to the local florist or from roadside stalls, through to large companies with broadacre plantations of thousands of plants.

Due to their adaptability for floral work and their long-lasting qualities proteas have been in great demand both on the local and overseas flower markets. Some outrageous claims about profitability on the cut flower market have been made by unscrupulous investment companies over recent years. The decision to grow proteas for commercial purposes must take many factors into account.

If you wish to grow proteas for the local or export market you must first decide where and how you are going to market your blooms.

Marketing Your Proteas

Local florists

These are usually a great market for small growers. The florists appreciate the individual service and the freshness of the flowers. Each florist should be consulted individually to discover what types of bloom and foliage they prefer as each may have their own speciality or style. Keeping bloom quality high is important to keep your customers happy. Poor quality, damaged or old blooms will soon lose you your local customers. Florists will usually require a wide range of different colours, flower types and foliage in a fairly constant supply. A very mixed protea plantation will be required to keep even one florist supplied. Growers supplying local florists directly need to be able to keep up the supply year round and must plan and plant accordingly.

Local floral artists

Floral artists are a great direct sales market for smaller protea growers. A general mixed plantation is required; however floral artists often seek out the more unusual or highly ornamental species for their work. An example of this is *Protea cynaroides* (king protea) which is sold in large quantities for export but usually has poor local sales. It is nevertheless a favourite of floral artists either in the bud or full bloom stages. The same is true of *Leucadendron argenteum* (silver tree) which has highly ornamental silver foliage. Floral artists may also be interested in dried protea flowers or even fresh or dried leucadendron cones.

Contact with local floral art societies and craft clubs or newspaper advertisements are probably the best ways to access this market.

Wholesalers

The wholesale market is extremely unreliable and very unpredictable. There is no guarantee that the flowers or foliage that are in great demand this year will be sought after in the next. With annual flowers this may not be a problem but with proteas which take up to five years to produce quality blooms this can cause great difficulty.

Most larger wholesalers deal with both the local floristry industry and the export market. They will generally require very high quality blooms in very large quantities. Advice must be sought from the wholesaler's marketing manager as to the varieties which should be planted and the quantities required. Generally the prices given by the wholesaler are much lower then can be obtained through direct sales. Wholesalers usually pay the grower about 70–80 per cent of the current market price. This is of course offset by the large quantities which the wholesaler is capable of handling.

Wholesalers may have special requirements such as:

1. Long stem length,
2. Superior bloom quality,
3. Very straight stems,
4. Fumigation,
5. Conditioning treatments (to increase flower life),
6. Coolroom storage,
7. Specific packaging.

Wholesalers should be contacted directly to obtain all the required information.

A growers co-operative

A growers co-operative is an excellent way for a group of smaller growers to market their product. A co-operative may be formed under the appropriate government legislation and provides many advantages for the small (or large) grower.

Some of the advantages of selling through a co-operative:

1. Increased volume and improved continuity of supply, making access to wholesalers possible.
2. Shared expertise, e.g. cultural or financial management.
3. Sharing of large capital expenditure items, e.g. packing sheds, cool rooms, machinery.
4. Bulk purchase of materials, e.g. packaging, chemicals, weedmat, plants.
5. Joint marketing, i.e. reduced grower to grower competition.

Direct sales/roadside stalls

Direct sales to the public depend very much on access to a sizable market. For a grower in a remote country area this may be very impractical, but a grower close to a large town or city may find direct sales an excellent source of income. Obviously advertising in local newspapers and magazines or on radio stations will greatly aid direct sales.

Access to direct delivery or direct pick-up is also very important for direct sales. This is where the roadside flower stall has its uses. On busy city access roads a roadside stall may be busy enough to clear all the grower's stock. The appropriate local government permits must be obtained.

Supermarkets

The sale of cut flowers and bunches of flowers through supermarkets is a growing trend world wide. Already supermarket sales account for a large percentage of flower sales in the USA.

Supermarkets are a great potential market for small to medium-scale growers who can keep up a constant year-round supply of flowers. Supermarkets will usually sell either individual cut flowers, small bunches of foliage or mixed bunches. The grower should contact the local supermarket, or if it belongs to a large chain of stores, the chain's wholesale buying division.

Generally a medium-sized mixed plantation based on the most popular cultivars will supply the required blooms for supermarket trade. Added costs will include time for making up bunches, weekly or bi-weekly deliveries and plastic sleeves, bands etc.

Establishment Costs

Once you have decided to go ahead with your commercial plantation some of the establishment and on-going costs must be considered.

A general list of costs to be considered may include:

1. Land purchase.
2. Packing shed, workshop, coolroom.
3. Machinery—tractor, mower, delivery van, tools.
4. Irrigation—equipment, water costs.

5. Fencing.
6. Plants—initial planting and replacement plants.
7. Chemicals—sprays, fertilisers, disinfectants.
8. Office equipment—computer, answering machine, fax.
9. Postage, telephone, electricity.
10. Labour.
11. Insurance.
12. Fuel/delivery costs.
13. Packaging materials.
14. Memberships/licence fees—co-operative fees, protea growers asssociation, local government fees.

Summary

After considering the possible means of marketing your produce and balancing it against the possible costs involved you will be ready to make the decision on your commercial protea plantation. The cut flower market has always been a risky business but it can also be very satisfying. To be able to give people the pleasure of fresh flowers and make an income at the same time is many people's idea of the perfect occupation.

Picking and Handling Proteas

Picking proteas

Only mature protea buds should be picked. Immature protea flower buds will not open and immature leucadendron stems will tend to wilt or blacken quickly. Mature protea flowers will have a few bracts just opening at the top. Leucospermums should be picked when 20–70 per cent of the styles have opened. Leucadendrons are ready to pick when the bracts have a firm, more leathery feel. Do not pick leucadendrons when they have soft feathery new growth as this will tend to wilt and blacken.

Early morning is the best time to pick as the plants are still cool and have replenished themselves with water overnight. If the blooms or foliage are still wet from overnight rain or dew they should be dried before being placed in the coolroom or packaging.

The blooms should always be cut using sharp clean secateurs, the bypass variety being the best. The general rules discussed in the pruning section should be applied to cutting the stems.

After picking, the blooms should be laid carefully in either baskets, picking boxes, wheelbarrows or even directly into water-filled buckets if appropriate transport is possible. The blooms should be taken directly to the handling shed in warm weather and should not be left in the plantation for more than 20–30 minutes. Cutting down the time between picking and placement in water will greatly extend the bloom life.

An initial sorting process should take place while picking. An obviously worthless bloom should be cut from the plant and discarded. Twisted, bent, damaged or low-quality blooms or short-stemmed blooms should be removed from the plant. It is pointless and time consuming carrying these back to the handling area. This also gives the plant an initial pruning.

Handling and storing proteas

In the packing and handling area a large table or bench is needed to sort the blooms out. Unmarketable, damaged or obviously unsuitable stems should be immediately discarded.

Usually the leaves on the lower half or one-third of the stem are removed. This reduces water loss through transpiration and prevents leaves being underwater while in storage. Stripping of the leaves is usually done by hand. It can be quickly achieved by firmly grasping the stem between the thumb and forefinger and dragging the stem quickly through. Care must be taken not to damage the stem as this will reduce the flower quality.

Stems should then be graded according to how you are marketing your flowers. For export the blooms and leaves need to be perfectly unblemished and disease free. The stems should be almost perfectly straight and the required length. Clarity and depth of colour may also be an important factor.

Once the blooms have been sorted into the appropriate grades they should be placed in water as soon as possible. Whether or not to recut the stems underwater is a point of argument among many growers. The idea is that this practice re-opens the stem's water passages without an airlock, allowing water to move into the stem more easily.

Premature blackening of the leaves is a serious problem faced by the growers and wholesalers of proteas. Those especially effected by this are

Protea neriifolia, P. repens, P. eximia and *P. compacta*. This blackening is brought about by natural chemical processes within the leaves: enzymes within the leaf cell begin to break down certain substances which causes the leaf to quickly loose colour and turn brown or black.

High temperatures and dehydration are seen as the major causes of leaf blackening. When the freshly cut stems are first placed in water they release phenolic compounds which, when taken back into the stem, will also accelerate leaf blackening. The water should be changed regularly to prevent this, especially in the first 12 hours.

Conditioning proteas

There has been considerable controversy and argument over whether attempting to condition proteas to extend their vase life is worthwhile. The latest research seems to have found that conditioning will extend vase life by up to 20 per cent. It may at least be useful in reducing the occurrence of premature leaf blackening in susceptible varieties.

The commercially available conditioning mixtures seem to be quite effective. A possible recipe for your own conditioning agent is:

Chlorine 8 gm/litre (or similar germicide)
Sugar 20 gm/litre
Citric acid 0.25 gm/litre (or silver thiosulphate salt)

After the blooms have been allowed to sit in the conditioner/water mix at room temperature for 3–4 hours the containers can be shifted to a coolroom if available. The optimum coolroom temperature seems to be in the range of 2–4°C. Air circulation within the coolroom also seems to be an advantage. Forcing cool air through the cut flowers will cool them quickly preventing the time lag to low temperature produced when a large quantity of room temperature flowers are first added to the coolroom.

Cold storage will keep proteas adequately for up to two weeks which is a great advantage when a large quantity of blooms is required for a single large-scale shipment.

Packaging

Flowers are usually carefully packed in corrugated cardboard flower boxes. They are packed in head to tail to allow a greater number to be placed in the one box.

A plastic or waxed paper liner may be used to prevent moisture loss. Newspaper can also be used to line the box or separate layers of flowers. For leucospermums a final fine spray of water before the lid is sealed helps prevent dehydration of the styles. When packing leucospermums great care must be taken not to tangle the styles as this will often cause them to break when being unpacked. For export the boxes may also have to be fumigated with an insecticide.

Drying Proteas

Proteas have been a very popular dried flower for many years. Most have some value as a dried flower, however the most popular proteas to dry are: *Protea neriifolia, P. cynaroides, P. repens, Leucadendron* 'Silvan Red', *L.* 'Safari Sunset', *L. gandogeri* and all the leucadendrons which produce prominant cones, e.g. *L. conicum, L. coniferum, L. eucalyptifolium, L. argenteum.*

Proteas may be simply air dried either in a vase with no water or hanging upside down. In either case direct light will fade the colour considerably so a dark shed or room is suitable. The material should be kept dry to prevent fungal growth. The plants may also be treated with glycerine before drying which gives the foliage more strength.

A mixture of one part glycerine to three parts water for 3–4 days seems ideal. Artificial fabric dyes may also be used in the glycerine mixture if required.

6 Proteas for Special Uses

Attracting Birds

Most proteas attract birds to some extent, especially nectar-feeding birds such as honeyeaters and wattlebirds.

Some of the more densely growing leucadendrons and proteas also make excellent shelter and nesting sites for such birds as thornbills and robins which mainly feed on insects attracted to the colour and nectar of the proteas.

In their native southern Africa many proteas and leucospermums rely on nectar-feeding birds and rodents for pollination.

The following proteas are the best for attracting birds:

Protea	*Leucospermum*
repens (especially rich in nectar)	All species are excellent.
'Pink Ice'	
longifolia	*Leucadendron*
cynaroides	*orientale*
obtusifolia	*uliginosum*
	daphnoides
	tinctum

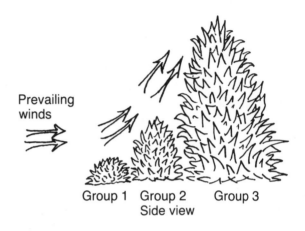

Group 1   Group 2   Group 3
Side view

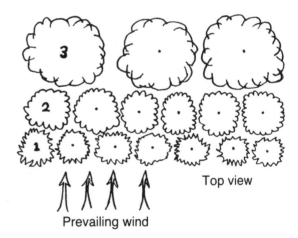

Prevailing wind   Top view

A possible windbreak design using Proteas

Windbreaks

Many of the taller and denser proteas make excellent windbreaks. Due to the varying sizes and habits of proteas it is possible to have a beautiful windbreak of many different protea types which also provide cut flowers and foliage.

A possible windbreak design:
   Group 1—low and bushy
   Group 2—medium and dense
   Group 3—tall

Group 1

Leucospermum 'Firewheel'	*Leucadendron gandogeri*
Leucospermum catherinae	*Leucadendron daphnoides*
Leucospermum lineare	*Leucadendron orientale*
Leucadendron discolor	

Group 2
Leucadendron laureolum
Leucadendron 'Silvan Red'
Leucadendron salignum
Leucospermum reflexum
Protea 'Pink Ice'
Protea neriifolia

Group 3
Protea repens
Leucadendron conicum
Leucadendron eucalyptifolium
Leucadendron meridianum
Leucadendron salicifolium
Leucadendron macowanii

Acid and Alkaline Soils

Proteas thrive in slightly acid to acid soils of about pH 5–6. Many proteas, however, will grow quite happily in slightly alkaline soils (pH above 7).

Species tolerant of alkaline soils

Protea	*Leucadendron*
'Pink Ice'	*laureolum*
neriifolia	*salignum*
obtusifolia	'Silvan Red'
burchelli	'Safari Sunset'
repens	*coniferum*
suzannae	Various cultivars of
	L. salignum

Leucospermum
cordifolium
'Firewheel'
patersonii

Frost Tolerance

Most proteas will tolerate light frosts. Severe frosts will often burn soft new growth, but this often has little more affect on the plant than pruning it. Frost-burnt growth should not be pruned off until after the danger of frost has passed as it helps protect the rest of the plant from further frost burn.

New young plants may be killed by frosts and can be protected with hessian or shadecloth covers.

The most frost-resistant species

Protea	*Leucadendron*
aristata	'Silvan Red' and other
'Pink Ice'	*L. salignum* hybrids
repens	*salignum*
eximia	*eucalyptifolium*
grandiceps	*salicifolium*
punctata	*Leucospermum*
magnifica	*catherinae*
	lineare

Poor Drainage

Most proteas require good drainage, but some species are quite tolerant if the soil is well drained for most of the year. Drainage can always be improved by using raised beds or even just mounding a few centimeters above normal ground level.

Proteas tolerant of poor drainage

Protea	*Leucadendron*
cynaroides	*salignum*
repens	*macowanii*
'Pink Ice'	*salignum* hybrids (e.g.
Leucospermum	'Silvan Red', 'Safari
'Firewheel'	Sunset')
	salicifolium
	uliginosum

Coastal Areas

Many proteas grow naturally near the coast in South Africa and are tolerant of salt-laden winds. The growth habit may of course be affected, and plants usually grow lower and slower on the coast than elsewhere.

Protea	*Leucadendron*
cynaroides	*argenteum*
compacta	*coniferum*
neriifolia	*eucalyptifolium*
'Pink Ice'	*floridum*
repens	*galpini*
burchelli	*gandogeri*
coronata	*laureolum*
grandiceps	*salignum*
lepidocarpodendron	*salignum* cultivars and
longifolia	hybrids
	sessile

Protea aurea   *Protea burchelli*   *Protea compacta*

Protea coronata   *Protea cynaroides*

Protea cynaroides in bud   *Protea eximia*   *Protea grandiceps*

Protea laurifolia (pink)   *Protea laurifolia* (cream)   *Protea lepidocarpodendron*

Protea longifolia (green)   *Protea longifolia* (cream)

Protea magnifica (cream)   *Protea magnifica* (pink)

Protea neriifolia (pink)

Protea neriifolia (cream)

Protea obtusifolia (white)

Protea obtusifolia (red)

Protea repens (white)

Protea repens (red)

Protea repens, fully blown stage

Protea scolymocephala

Protea 'Pink Ice'

Protea 'Frosted Fire'

Leucadendron argenteum tree

Leucadendron argenteum foliage

Leucadendron conicum (male)

Leucadendron conicum, late cone stage (female)

Leucadendron daphnoides   *Leucadendron discolor* (male)   *Leucadendron discolor* (female)

Leucadendron eucalyptifolium, view of whole shrub   *Leucadendron eucalyptifolium* foliage

Leucadendron gandogeri   *Leucadendron globosum*

37

Leucadendron lanigerum

Leucadendron laureolum (male)

Leucadendron laureolum (female)

Leucadendron orientale, early green stage

Leucadendron orientale, later yellow stage

Leucadendron rubrum

38

Leucadendron salicifolium, early flowering stage

Leucadendron salignum, red-flowered, low form

Leucadendron salignum, red-flowering low form at the late winter colour stage

Leucadendron salignum, red-flowering, tall form

Leucadendron salignum, yellow form

Leucadendron stroblinum (male)

Leucadendron stroblinum (male), view of whole shrub

Leucadendron stroblinum (female)

39

Leucadendron stelligerum

Leucadendron uliginosum

Leucadendron brunioides

Leucadendron xanthaconus,
cone stage

Leucadendron 'Silvan Red', early autumn
coloration

Leucadendron 'Silvan Red', later
colour stage

Leucadendron 'Safari Sunset'

Leucadendron 'Red Devil'

Leucadendron 'Yellow Crest'

Leucospermum
mundii
patersonii
reflexum
tottum

Commercial Cut Flowers and Foliage

Most proteas can be used for fresh cut flowers or foliage. Many are also very attractive when dried. However, some species are much more suitable than others due to longer stem length, longer vase life or more attractive foliage when dried. The following lists contain the protea species that have consistently proved the most popular with florists and floral artists.

Protea
'Pink Ice'
longifolia
repens
compacta
neriifolia
cynaroides
magnifica
grandiceps
speciosa
obtusifolia
aristata
burchelli
coronata
'Clarks Red'
laurifolia
stokoei
punctata
scolymocephala
lepidocarpodendron

Leucadendron
argenteum
daphnoides
discolor
floridum
laureolum
rubrum
procerum
'Silvan Red'
'Safari Sunset'
'Red Gem'
orientale
salignum (and all cultivars)
platyspermum
thymifolium
tinctum
xanthaconus
galpini
macowanii
eucalyptifolium
conicum
gandogeri
coniferum
salicifolium
uliginosum

Leucospermum
catherinae
cordifolium (and cultivars and hybrids)
conocarpodendron
lineare
tottum
reflexum
patersonii
glabrum
vestitum

Proteas Suitable for Growing in Tubs

Many proteas are suitable for growing in large tubs and the most suitable are listed below. Remember many of these may require heavy pruning to prevent them becoming too large.

Protea
scolymocephela
cynaroides (dwarf variety)
nana

Leucospermum
cordifolium (all varieties)
'Mardi Gras'
'Firewheel'
'Scarlet Ribbon'
lineare
conocarpodendron
tottum

Leucadendron
salignum (all varieties)
'Yellow Crest'
'Red Devil'
brunioides
daphnoides
discolor
gandogeri
orientale
thymifolium

41

7 Descriptions of Species and Cultivars

Author's note

The number of *Protea* species and those of related genera is enormous so only the most commonly grown species and hybrids are described here. Also, the common names of many proteas vary. This is especially so for the hybrids which are often named differently according to the whims of the nursery industry.

There are also many names used by the nursery trade for 'selected' or 'new varieties' which are in fact just naturally occurring colour or habit variations of one of the standard species. The names used in this section are to the best of my knowledge the most commonly used at the time of publication.

Genus *Protea*

Protea aristata

This protea has not been given the recognition and is not grown as widely as it deserves.

The plant shows a very neat upright habit and produces long-stemmed bright pink to red-crimson flowers. The flower bracts are covered with fine hairs, giving a lovely soft silvery appearance which further enhances the flower.

P. aristata flowers throughout late spring and summer when many other proteas have finished flowering.

The leaves are blue-green and needle-like, thickly crowded along the stems pointing upwards.

This is a slow-growing protea reaching 1.5 m in height and 1 m in width.

P. aristata makes an excellent cut flower or garden plant and is quite frost hardy.

Protea aurea

This is a tall shrub which grows to 3.5 m in height and 2 m in width.

The flower buds are quite unusual being about the size and shape of an adult's finger. Once the flower opens it quickly spreads and may become very messy and untidy in appearance. This process is often hastened by visits from nectar-feeding birds and bees.

There are many different flowering forms from shades of cream, through pinks, crimsons and red. A few flowers may appear at any time of the year however the main flowering period is autumn and winter.

The leaves are oval and stiff and leathery to feel. The young leaves and new shoots are usually very soft and silvery in appearance.

This is a very adaptable protea and is hardy to most soil and weather conditions provided it has reasonable drainage. It may tend to grow a little quickly and become tall and straggly and should be pruned back after flowering. This will keep the shrub a little lower and bushier in shape and will also produce a lot more flower heads in the next season.

Protea burchelli

Protea burchelli has proved to be a quite hardy and easily grown protea both for the home gardener and the cut flower grower. It grows to about 1.5 m to 2 m high and 1.5 m across and is usually quite bushy even without pruning.

The flowers vary in colour from deep red through pale pinks to cream. The bracts are often quite shiny and the tips are fringed with fine black hairs. The main flowering time is late winter and spring.

P. burchelli is tolerant of a wide range of soil types and conditions, including long dry spells. Cuttings from semi-hardwood strike easily and it is also easily grown from seed.

Although popular with florists *P. burchelli* flowers tend to open out very quickly after picking; however, their smaller size and very distinct coloration make them an excellent cut flower.

Protea compacta ('The Prince Protea')

P. compacta is a very popular cut flower and if pruned regularly makes an excellent garden plant.

The bushes grow to a height of 3 m if left unpruned, which often results in a few sparse long straggly stems and flowers too high to be seen and difficult to pick. This protea should be pruned back regularly to increase the number of stems and keep it to a more convenient height.

P. compacta produces very neat small pointed bracts which open quickly to a goblet-like shape. The flowers are usually a soft but bright pink and there is also a cream form. Flowering occurs over a long period from autumn through to mid-summer. The main flowering time is usually mid-winter.

The new shoots are usually very soft and feathery and may be susceptible to frost attack. The mature leaves are however quite stout and leathery and are quite frost resistant. Leaves lower on the stems often become diseased due to fungus attack and may become unsightly.

P. compacta does require well drained soils but is quite hardy once established.

The flowers are very popular with florists and floral artists due to their compact nature and long stem length, but they do have a shorter vase life than some of the other proteas. *P. compacta* also makes an excellent landscaping plant due to its tall slender growth and lovely soft blue-green foliage.

Protea coronata (The 'Green Protea')

The distinctive feature of this protea is the bright apple-green colour of the flowers. The bush itself often tends to be tall and straggly and should be kept pruned to produce a better shrub.

The flowers are cup-shaped with a white (or more rarely pink) woolly centre protuding from the bracts. The leaves are a soft grey-green and often cover most of the flower. The main flowering time is winter to late spring.

P. coronata is quite easily grown but the leaves tend to be susceptible to fungal attack which causes them to become black and untidy in appearance.

If well pruned *P. coronata* will grow to a bushy 3 m with a width of 3 m. It is an excellent garden plant and the distinctive green flowers on long stems are popular with floral artists. This is a great plant for protea collectors because it is the only truly green protea flower.

Protea cynaroides (The King Protea)

This is probably the best known of all the protea family. The flowers can be up to 30 cm in diameter on up to 1 m stems and are very popular on the international flower market.

The plant tends to be quite untidy due to the nature of the stem growth. King proteas have a lignotuber (or underground trunk) and the flower shoots grow straight from the lignotuber. With careful, though severe, pruning the plant can be made to produce a shrub of sorts but the best method for flower production is to cut off the flower stems flush with the ground.

Many gardeners complain about the untidiness of the plant but this is really its natural appearance and the flowers are worth the untidy plant. Another problem many gardeners have is that their large healthy king protea refuses to flower even after many years. This may be due to excess growth due to high nitrogen levels in the soil. This may correct itself in time. The best method to induce flowering is to cut all the stems back to the trunk, flush with ground level. This can be done with large pruners or a small hand saw. New shoots will soon appear and these will usually produce a flower in 12-18 months.

King proteas thrive in most well drained acid soils, however they do require a little more water than most other species.

There are four main types of king protea. These flower at different times of the year (summer, autumn, winter, spring) and also have slightly different flowers and leaf shape. The autumn/winter flowering type has a distinctive round bud about the size of a large apple. The colours vary from a deep pink/red through pinks to a very pale creamy pink.

For the home gardener interested in proteas

a king protea in their collection is essential. If you have a good nursery you may be able to obtain variants which flower during each season. This, however, is often pot luck as nursery plants are usually 100 per cent seed grown and their flowering season can only be guessed at. Because of their untidy nature it is best to plant three or four (or more if you have the space) king proteas within a 2 m circle and let them intertwine. This will produce a magnificent display of flowers.

As a cut flower the king protea stands literally above all others. It has a vase life of many weeks if the water is changed regularly. Two or three king protea flowers in a large floral arrangement are quite spectacular. They also dry reasonably well and are often used in this manner.

The only major disease of king proteas is leaf spotting which is caused by fungal attack and shows as ugly red or brown spots on the leaves. This is difficult to combat once the spots appear but early treatment with a general fungicide will probably prevent it spreading to all the leaves.

Protea eximia (The Duchess Protea)

This is a widely cultivated and generally hardy garden plant. *P. eximia* is not highly rated as a cut flower as the bracts tend to open quickly and the inner flower parts spread out to become untidy. Leaf blackening after cutting also occurs more rapidly than in other species.

P. eximia grows to about 2 m in height and width. It forms a fairly dense bush but it may become untidy in old age if it is not pruned regularly.

The flowers are quite large, approximately 15 cm long and up to 20 cm in width when open. The colour varies from light pink to dark crimson bracts with dark crimson centre. Flowers are carried on the bush all year round, although the main flowering time is winter.

The leaves are quite large, up to 60 mm in diameter, and may have a crimson tinge to their colour at certain times of the year.

P. eximia has proved to be very easily grown in most areas provided it has reasonable drainage. In cooler, moist climates, however, it often suffers from blackening of the lower leaves on the stems and internal parts of the bush.

It is a very useful garden specimen being compact, easily grown and carrying flowers for 12 months of the year.

Protea grandiceps (The 'Princess Protea')

One of the most beautiful protea flowers, *P. grandiceps* is not widely found in home gardens. The flowers are quite large, up to 16 cm in length and 8–10 cm in width. They are usually a very striking red-pink colour with snowy white or white and brown fringes to the bracts. The flower head is quite tightly formed and stays this way even after weeks in a vase. Flowers appear from late winter to early summer.

The leaves are large and leathery with a pink to red margin and often a red tinge.

The plant tends to spread out to about 2 m in width with a height of about 1.5 m but is very slow growing. If desired, stems which grow parallel to the ground should be pruned off to force the plant to a more upright bushy form.

P. grandiceps is quite easily grown in most well drained acid soils, however new growth may be burnt off by frosts. It is also a popular haunt for many types of small spiders which make their home in the densely packed leaves. Some gardeners may see this as an advantage as the flower spiders are often brightly coloured and quite harmless.

P. grandiceps is a spectacular garden specimen with its lovely blue-green foliage and large striking flowers. It is also an excellent cut flower with long thick flower stems and a very long vase life. This is a highly recommended species.

Protea holisericea

This unusual but extremely attractive protea features large cream flowers with black-fringed bracts.

The shrub tends to be a sprawling 2 × 2 m plant which needs to be kept well pruned when young to keep a good form. The flowers appear in late spring and summer. *P. holisericea* needs very good drainage and the leaves can become discoloured by fungal attack in more humid climates.

P. holisericea makes an excellent specimen plant in any garden and the blooms, although quite large, make excellent cut flowers.

Protea lacticolor

P. lacticolor is a tall slender shrub or small tree which in cultivation may reach a height of 4–5 m.

The flower buds are cylindrical to funnel shaped, opening quickly to an open funnel-shaped flower. The flower may open even further and become untidy when visited by bees and nectar-feeding birds. Flower colour varies from cream to a bright pink. The main flowering period is autumn to early winter.

The leaves are a distinctive blue-green colour and quite stiff and thick. They are oval shaped with a slight point.

P. lacticolor is a very useful and easy-to-grow garden plant in most well drained situations. Its distinctive foliage and slender habit make it an excellent landscaping plant.

The flowers are popular with floral artists but do not have a long vase life and tend to open out very quickly.

Protea laurifolia

This outstanding protea is often confused with *P. neriifolia*. Although the flowers are quite similar, *P. laurifolia* has distinctive large, thick blue-green leaves and a large, more rounded flower.

P. laurifolia can grow to a height of 3 × 2 m with strong upright stems. The flowers vary from a beautiful dusty pink to a rather unattractive dirty cream colour with a soft black fringe. Flowers may be present all year round although the main flowering period is from late autumn to early spring. They can be quite large, up to 13 cm long and 8 cm in diameter.

P. laurifolia is usually an easy protea to grow once established. Pruning the plant continually when it is young is important to stop it becoming too straggly and untidy.

This protea produces long-stemmed flowers which have excellent vase life. The soft pink variants are very popular with floral artists because of their lovely soft-coloured foliage. There is some problem with leaf blackening after picking so care must be taken to change the vase water regularly, adding a teaspoon of bleach to reduce bacterial and fungal growth.

P. laurifolia makes an excellent specimen plant for the garden with its striking foliage and long flowering season.

P. lepidocarpodendron ('The Black Protea')

This is a most unusual protea with its black and dark purple flowers. The flowers are often almost covered by the leaves which should be thinned out around the flower after picking to reveal the flower head.

This is an interesting specimen plant due to its distinctive colouring, plants with truly black flowers being rare in nature. The flowers are similar in size and shape to *P. neriifolia* but are a little smaller and more slender. They are unusually black at the top fading to a light purple at the base. The bracts are fringed with white and cover a white central flower mass.

P. lepidocarpodendron produces flowers from late autumn through winter to early summer with the peak flowering time being mid-winter.

This protea is reasonably easy to grow in most situations although it may be frost tender when young or when carrying a lot of new growth. The flowers are carried on long stems to 50 cm making it an excellent cut flower.

The shrub grows to about 3 m in height and 1.5 m in width and is quite neat and erect making it an excellent specimen plant for home gardens. As with most other proteas careful pruning is required when young to produce a more pleasing plant shape and more flowers.

Protea longifolia

This is a very popular and easily grown protea. The flowers are quite large and elegant in shape with long slender leaves and vary in colour from a soft lime green to a pinkish cream colour.

Once established, *P. longifolia* is a hardy and very attractive garden plant. Its flowers also produce large amounts of nectar and like all green flowers are powerful bird attracters.

The flowers are quite waxy in texture with a beautiful protruding central part to the flower which is usually white, fringed with black. The leaves are long and slender (hence the name) and deep green.

The flowers are very popular with floral artists but they are rarely found in large quantities on the cut flower market. The shrub is open and upright and grows to about 2 m in height and approximately 1.5 m in width. The flowers are present all year round except summer, with the main flowering in mid-winter.

Protea magnifica (The Queen Protea)

A very well known and popular protea which was previously called *P. barbigera*, the queen protea produces the second largest protea flowers, up to 15 cm in length and width. These magnificent flowers vary in colour from a soft cream through a range of pinks to a deep pink/red. Each flower bract has it own tuft of white or fawn hair on the bract tips and a fringe of white or black around the opening. The central flower mass is white, with a white to dark purple centre.

The overall effect of this fringing gives a lovely soft appearance to the flower making it one of the most beautiful and appealing protea flowers.

The flowers are usually present from early winter through spring to early summer, although flowering times vary greatly with the different queen protea varieties.

The plants themselves vary greatly from straggly, rather untidy plants, spreading across the ground, to quite upright shrubs. With severe pruning while young, most queen protea plants can be forced into a reasonable shrub form. Any sideways or downward pointing branches should be removed. This will also encourage longer and straighter stems to form. Most plants tend to grow to about 2 m but are quite slow growing, taking many years to reach this height.

The queen protea is reasonably disease resistant once established but does suffer from leaf-eating insects and fungal spots on the leaves. Colourful flower spiders also enjoy making their homes on this protea; they are small and harmless.

The queen protea has proved a very popular cut flower on the international market due to its long, strong flower stems and long vase life. The large striking flowers are very popular with florists and floral artists, usually forming the main part of large vase arrangements.

When pruned correctly the queen protea makes an excellent garden plant and should always be included in any protea collection.

Protea mundii

This protea has unusual finger-shaped flower buds similar to *P. lacticolor* only slightly smaller. The flower buds open quickly and flatten out with the central flower bracts quickly becoming straggly and untidy. This happens especially quickly when the flower is visited by birds or bees.

The flowers vary in colour from a white cream through to a soft pink. Most varieties are in the pink colour range. The flowers are present from late summer through to mid-winter with the main flowering in autumn.

P. mundii may grow to a slender tree of about 10 m in height, however most specimens in cultivation reach a maximum of 5 m with a width of about 3 m.

This protea makes an excellent garden specimen with its lovely blue-green foliage and interesting flowers. The flowers tend to open too quickly to make it a popular flower with florists, however buds are quite often used.

P. mundii has proven quite hardy but should be kept pruned to a shorter, sturdier habit otherwise it may be susceptible to blowing over in windy areas.

Protea nana (Mountain Rose Protea)

One of the smaller protea varieties, *P. nana* is a most suitable plant for small gardens. Its appearance is quite different from that of many of the other proteas, its fine needle-like leaves and smaller cup-shaped flowers which tend to droop on the longer flower stems giving it quite a graceful look.

The flowers usually appear from early winter to the end of spring and are a beautiful deep red-claret colour. The shrub has quite upright stems, growing to about 0.75–1 m in height and up to 1 m in width.

P. nana has proved to be fairly short lived and seems quite susceptible to soil-borne fungal diseases such as *Phytophthora* (cinnamon fungus) which causes root rot. It seems to be best suited to cooler climates and is quite frost resistant.

P. nana has not commonly been grown commercially, probably due to the droopy nature of the flowers, but makes an excellent smaller garden specimen and is most useful in landscape design. The flowers also last quite well and make excellent cut flowers for the home gardener or enthusiast.

Protea neriifolia (Pink Mink, White Mink)

P. neriifolia is probably the most widely grown and easily recognised protea of all.

Its popularity is probably due to the fact that it adapts to most soils and situations, is resistant to most diseases and is quite frost resistant. *P. neriifolia* also flowers for most of the year depending on the variety.

The flowers all have the distinctive 'beard' on the tips of the bracts, usually black but sometimes brown or frosty white. The flowers are very variable in size, shape and colour. The most common colour type is a deep pink, however the colours range from a wine red through all shades of pink to cream.

Flower shapes vary from quite cone shaped to oblong or even egg shaped. The flowers can be from 60 mm to 150 mm in length and are usually terminal on long stems. The leaves are usually quite long (up to 150 mm) and either a bright green or blue-green. Most shrubs grow to about 2.5 × 2.5 m when fully mature.

P. neriifolia and all its variants are very easy to grow. It is quite frost hardy and grows in a range of soil types and soil acidities. It can tolerate fairly wet conditions and will even grow in some heavier clay soils.

The many variants of *P. neriifolia* flower at all times of the year although most of the flowering is in autumn, winter and spring. Mature bushes, however, are rarely without a flower.

P. neriifolia does need regular pruning to keep it from becoming straggly, especially while the plant is young. Old flower heads should all be removed.

P. neriifolia is a very popular cut flower for commercial purposes and is widely grown for the cut flower trade. It is also a very popular garden plant.

Protea obtusifolia

This protea is one of the few that will tolerate quite alkaline soils up to pH 8. This means it can be grown by gardeners who have failed to grow other proteas due to alkaline soils, such as occur in limestone areas on the coast.

P. obtusifolia has quite striking white, cream or deep red flowers which have a waxy sheen to the bracts. The flowers are most common in autumn and winter with some persisting until spring. The flowers are oblong-oval or goblet shaped and up to 10 cm in length. The leaves have a distinctly rounded tip and are a deep green.

P. obtusifolia is quite easily grown in most garden situations and is excellent for windy coastal situations. It is quite disease resistant but tends to be frost sensitive, especially when the plants are actively growing (autumn and spring).

The better colour forms are very popular as both commercial cut flower crops and garden specimen plants. The shrubs grow to about 3 m and are generally slow growing but will live for about 25–30 years on average.

Protea punctata

The most common colour form of this protea is a lovely soft pink which makes it a most attractive garden plant or cut flower. The small fingerlike buds open out quickly to display the actual flower parts. Unfortunately these often quickly become untidy due to bird or insect visits.

P. punctata also has very attractive blue-green, almost circular leaves which distinguish this species from the very similar *P. mundii* and *P. lacticolor*. It grows to a slender 2–3 m in height and needs to be pruned regularly to keep it from becoming too sparse in growth.

This is a reasonably easy protea to grow but does require a well drained site and likes to be in a well ventilated sunny position.

The flowers appear in late summer and autumn and need to be picked as buds and allowed to open after picking. This prevents insects or birds damaging the flower centre.

Protea repens (Honey Protea)

This has been a very popular protea for many years and was one of the first proteas to be widely cultivated outside South Africa. *P. repens* is a large, vigorous and very long-lived protea, however it does become straggly with age.

The plants vary from 2–3 m in width and height to a small bushy tree up to 4–5 m in height. The leaves are quite distinct: smooth, long and narrow and usually a light green colour.

The flowers vary in colour from a claret red through a range of pinks to rich creams and even snowy white. The bracts are often mostly white with attractive pink or red tips.

The flowers have a waxy appearance due to the abundant nectar which they produce, hence their common name the honey protea. This copious flow of nectar makes them great attracters of insects and birds which eat insects or nectar. The flowers need to be picked in the bud stage otherwise they become badly damaged by insects and birds feeding on them.

The main flowering time is autumn and winter, although there are selections which will flower in late summer. These late summer-flowering varieties are, however, often quite straggly with poor flower stem length.

P. repens has proved very easy to grow in a wide variety of soil types and climates. It is also one of the proteas more tolerant of alkaline soils and this, along with its hardy nature, make it ideal for coastal gardens.

P. repens has proved quite disease resistant although young plants may suffer some fungal disease of the foliage.

The commercial value of *P. repens* has been widely recognised by the cut flower industry for many years and it is widely grown for both local and international markets.

P. repens has strong straight stems and an excellent vase life. It also tends to flower earlier than many other popular commercial varieties. It is a popular screen plant for gardens, especially for those who wish to attract birds to their garden.

Protea scolymocephala (Mini Protea)

A very dainty and beautiful small protea which has not as yet been widely cultivated outside South Africa.

The mini protea only grows to about 1 m in height and a similar width and bears numerous small flowers which are not unlike tiny king protea flowers.

The flowers are most commonly a bright cream/green colour with pinkish tips to the bracts. There is, however, a most attractive variant which is mostly a crimson/red colour. The flowers are usually only about 3–4 cm wide and can be borne either in clusters or as single flower heads.

P. scolymocephala can be grown in a wide variety of soils but prefers lighter acidic types. Its low growth habit makes it suitable for coastal or windy spots and it does prefer an open sunny position.

Floral artists have found the delicate foliage and small dainty flowers make the mini protea an ideal cut flower for bouquet work, small sprays and smaller table arrangements. It is, however, not widely grown commercially.

P. scolymocephala is an outstanding small garden plant and grows beautifully in a large pot or cut-off wine barrel. It also blends in well with most cottage garden plants.

Protea speciosa

P. speciosa is one of the proteas which grows from a lignotuber (or underground trunk). It bears unusual flowers on long stems originating from the lignotuber. These are quite large, usually a light pink with attractive brown tufts of hair on the ends of the bracts.

The plant usually only grows to about 1 m in height and the flower stems may fall over and grow horizontally. The leaves are oval and quite large and leathery. Severe pruning while young will produce a more shrub-like habit.

Flowering time is from early winter to late spring with the main flowering in spring.

P. speciosa needs good drainage and open sunny spots and does not like constant humidity.

This protea has been grown in small quantities commercially and is a popular cut flower or specimen plant for the home gardener. It does suffer from fungal attack in more humid areas and also attack from leaf-eating insects.

Protea stokoei

P. stokoei has a most striking large flower head semi-enclosed by large leathery leaves with distinctive red borders. The most common colour is a lovely lustrous lipstick pink with soft brown hairy tips to the bracts. The large (up to 150 mm long) flower heads are carried on thick short stems and appear mainly in winter and early spring.

The plant only grows to a compact 1.5 m and is quite slow growing.

P. stokoei makes an excellent garden specimen plant and the cut flowers last well in a vase. It is often difficult to grow and requires a very well drained acid soil with a relatively high organic content.

Probably due to its shorter stem length and particular growth requirements *P. stokoei* has not been widely grown commercially. It does, however, make an excellent garden specimen plant and the spectacular flowers make it well worth the effort to grow.

Protea susannae

The main interest of *P. susannae* is that it is one of the few *Protea* species that will grow in quite alkaline soils as well as acid ones. It is also one of the largest proteas with shrubs growing to

Leucospermum catherinae

Leucospermum conocarpodendron

Leucospermum cordifolium, red form

Leucospermum reflexum, yellow form

Leucospermum reflexum, red form

Leucospermum tottum

Leucospermum 'Firewheel'

49

Leucospermum 'Scarlet Ribbon'

Serruria florida (Blushing Bride)

A *Leucadendron* 'Silvan Red' before pruning

Leucadendron 'Silvan Red' after pruning

Picking a *Protea* 'Pink Ice' flower; note approximately 10 cm of stem is left

New shoots appearing on *Protea* 'Pink Ice' shortly after flower picking

Open seed follicles on a *Leucadendron conicum* cone

Cuttings under a mist system in a polythene igloo

Diseased foliage of *Protea nerii-folia* caused by sooty mould

Leaf spot on *Protea cynaroides*

Leaf spot on *Protea eximia*

Yellowing of the leaves caused by iron deficiency in a young leucadendron plant

Frost damaged leaves on *Protea grandiceps*

If flowers are not picked when they first open bees will often quickly damage the internal flower parts

51

Leucadendron eucalyptifolium being used as a windbreak in a commercial plantation

A commercial plantation of *Protea cynaroides*

A commercial plantation of *Protea eximia*

A morning's picking of proteas ready for sorting

A *Leucospermum* 'Firewheel' being grown in a large plastic tub

A floral arrangement using leucospermums

Protea cynaroides and *Protea com* feature in a modern arrangement

about 3.5 m tall and 3.5 m wide.

The flowers are usually a dark red, often with a brownish fringe to the bracts. The bracts open wide quite quickly to reveal flower parts which become untidy, usually due to the activities of bees and birds. The main flowering period is autumn and winter.

P. susannae has proved a very easy garden plant to grow, tolerating a wide variety of conditions. It is a useful coastal garden plant, often growing where many other plants have failed, particularly in poor coastal sands.

Unfortunately *P. susannae* does not lend itself to being a cut flower as the leaves give off a rather pungent unpleasant odour. It does make an excellent, hardy garden plant especially useful for screening purposes in coastal gardens.

Protea 'Pink Ice' (hybrid)

This outstanding hybrid protea has become one of the world's leading cut flowers and makes an excellent showy and extremely hardy garden plant.

'Pink Ice' has superb soft to bright pink flowers with a slight white fringe which gives it a lovely 'frosted' appearance. The flower is quite compact and maintains its neat appearance for a long period of time after the bud opens, unless damaged by weather, insects or birds.

'Pink Ice' bushes rarely seem to be completely without flowers, with a good supply from autumn through to early summer. The flowers are almost always terminal and appear in great numbers on fully grown plants.

The bush can grow to about 2.5 m high and 2 m wide when fully grown. With a little pruning, especially when the plant is young, 'Pink Ice' usually maintains a fairly dense and compact shape. It does not tend to become straggly with age like many of the other protea species. Flowers should be picked from the bushes each year to encourage further bushy growth and even more flowers in the next season.

'Pink Ice' will grow well in a wide variety of soil types and climates. It is quite tolerant of alkaline soils and will tolerate quite heavy (even clay) soils. The compact, bushy habit of the shrub makes it a sturdy plant even in very windy rough sites. 'Pink Ice' has also proved to be very disease resistant. It tolerates long periods of waterlogged soils, resisting fungal root diseases better than all the protea species. It is also much less susceptible to fungal attack of the leaves and stems, even in humid conditions.

'Pink Ice' makes an outstanding cut flower and is grown extensively world wide by commercial growers. The flowers are carried on long, straight stems, have a very long vase life and survive long periods of transportation extremely well. They are very numerous on the plants which have an extended flowering season. 'Pink Ice' is very popular with florists and floral artists, not only for the lovely, long-lasting, soft pink, compact flowers but also for the soft green foliage. The blooms can be used in all types of arrangement from the largest display to smaller baskets or posies.

In the garden this protea has few equals either as a fine specimen plant or as a very attractive screen or windbreak.

'Pink Ice' propagates readily from semi-hardened cuttings taken in autumn and winter.

Protea 'Frosted Fire' (hybrid)

This is probably a hybrid between *P. neriifolia* and *P. longifolia*.

P. 'Frosted Fire', has lovely bright pink/red flowers with a white fringe which combines with a slight waxy appearance of the bracts to give the flower its 'frosted' appearance. The shrub grows to about 2 m high and 1.5 m wide and is quite neat and compact in shape. The young plant, like most proteas, does require tip pruning to encourage this bushy habit.

The leaves are somewhat similar to those of some of the *P. neriifolia* varieties, being rather narrow and stiff to touch. They are usually dark green or blue-green.

'Frosted Fire' flowers appear mainly from late autumn to late winter. They are very abundant on the bushes and tend to be much more conspicuous than those of *P. neriifolia*. It is quite common to have up to 25 blooms on plants only four years old.

'Frosted Fire', like most protea hybrids, is quite hardy in the garden, tolerating a wide variety of soil types and conditions. It does, however, much prefer an open, well ventilated site and has sometimes proved susceptible to fungal diseases of the leaves in humid, enclosed positions.

'Frosted Fire' makes an excellent cut flower

although achieving adequate stem length for the export market does seem to be a problem. The flowers are long lasting after picking and very popular with florists and floral artists due to the striking flower colour and bright foliage.

'Frosted Fire' also makes an excellent garden specimen and is ideal as a feature plant or as part of a larger collection for screening. It is, however, quite slow growing compared to its parent species. 'Frosted Fire' is also quite slow to strike from cuttings, often taking up to six months to set roots.

Genus *Leucadendron*

Leucadendrons are a very large and diverse genus of protea-type plants which vary from small trees and large, very bushy shrubs down to small groundcover-like plants.

A special characteristic of leucadendrons is that they have separate male and female plants. This often causes great disappointment when a seed-grown plant from a nursery does not turn out the same as the attractive colour tag. The male and female plants of some species are very different in appearance. Female plants develop large cones bearing seed after the flowering season. Only plants grown from cuttings guarantee the desired sex.

Leucadendron argenteum ('Silver Tree')

This is a most striking leucadendron due to its beautiful shining, shimmering foliage and makes a magnificent feature plant for any garden.

The leaves are long, soft and elegant in appearance with a soft silvery coating of hairs covering their surface. They are usually a light blue-green with the covering of hairs giving the characteristic shiny, metallic appearance.

The 'Silver Tree' grows to a slender 8-10 m in height and up to 3 m in width. The leaves are quite dense on the branches giving the tree a reasonably dense overall appearance.

The male flowers are yellow, usually appearing in spring. They are up to 50 mm in diameter and with the surrounding silver leaves are an attractive flower head on long stems.

The female cones are oval and a similar colour to the foliage. They may be found on the plant over many months and flower in spring.

The 'Silver Tree' has proved to be very unpredictable in cultivation. It has been grown successfully in a wide variety of soils but has a tendency to grow well for a number of years and then suddenly die for no apparent reason. Although the 'Silver Tree', like the other proteas, requires very good drainage it appears that it does require reasonable moisture in the soil at all times. For this reason it often does not grow well in poor, well drained sands which many other proteas flourish in.

The 'Silver Tree' should also be grown in a well ventilated position as the hairy leaves make it susceptible to leaf and black soot-type fungal diseases. It has also proved quite frost tender especially as a young plant.

L. argenteum is also one of the more difficult proteas to propagate from cuttings. Most propagation is carried out from seed which is very slow to germinate.

L. argenteum is a prized garden specimen plant for those who have successfully grown one. The foliage and flowers are used by florists and floral artists to striking effect in small and large arrangements. *L. argenteum* does not, however, have a long vase life compared to most other leucadendrons. The dried female cones are also used widely in floral art.

Leucadendron conicum

This large leucadendron grows to approximately 7 m tall and 3–4 m in diameter.

L. conicum has lovely soft dark green foliage. The small (20–30 mm long) leaves are often tinged with red around the edges and the newer stems are often a soft pink/red colour.

The new shoots are also often red tinged and they open to expose the cone surrounded by a pink/red star of small bracts. The shrub becomes covered with these in spring giving a most attractive display.

Although this flowering season is quite brief the foliage is highly sought after by florists at this time. It can be used for most of the year by florists or floral artists except when it is too soft after a growth spurt (usually early autumn).

This leucadendron needs to be cut back quite severely each year if it is to be useful for cut foliage as it will tend to become too tall and sparse at the top. Cutting back each year will encourage the growth of more bushy new foliage.

L. conicum has proved very hardy in most situations and a wide variety of soil types. It makes an excellent large screen plant or windbreak and is an extremely useful commercial leucadendron for cut foliage.

L. conicum is reasonably disease resistant but needs to be grown in a well ventilated spot to prevent mildew-type fungal attack. Some pruning away of thick undergrowth near the centre and base of the plant will also aid good ventilation.

Leucadendron coniferum

One of the few proteas that grows really well on alkaline soils, *L. coniferum* will even grow well in exposed coastal positions and makes an excellent seaside windbreak.

The foliage is a light green colour and the cones are surrounded by bright yellow-green bracts in late winter to mid-spring. The foliage is very popular with florists all year round but especially after flowering when the bright red female cones form. These also dry quite well.

L. coniferum grows to about 2 × 2 m and has proved very hardy and easy to grow. It can be pruned quite heavily to retain its bushy appearance. It is grown commercially for its fresh foliage and for dried material and makes an excellent garden plant.

Leucadendron daphnoides

This beautiful small leucadendron has been very popular in cultivation for many years. Like many of the other leucadendrons *L. daphnoides* passes through a series of colour changes. The bracts surrounding the flower cones begin the same colour as the rest of the leaves, a soft light green colour. They then turn a butter yellow to a very pale cream colour as the yellow central flower parts appear in late winter. This yellow colouring may persist throughout early spring but in most varieties it then changes to a soft red, blushed appearance. The intermediary stages between these colours are also very attractive and make this a most appealing leucadendron.

L. daphnoides only grows to approximately 1.5 × 1.5 m and is usually quite bushy and mound shaped in habit.

It makes an excellent cut flower especially with its range of colours and the lovely soft foliage on long straight stems. *L. daphnoides*, like all of the leucadendrons with soft hairy foliage, may be susceptible to some of the mildew-type fungal diseases if not in a well ventilated position. It is also quite frost tender, especially while the plants are young.

L. daphnoides makes a beautiful garden specimen plant especially for small gardens. It is also a popular cut flower but it does not have a long vase life.

Leucadendron discolor

This medium-sized leucadendron has one of the most spectacular flowers of this group. It is often sold under the name 'Flame-tips'. In spring the male flowers turn a bright flame red colour surrounded by yellow bracts. The flowers only last a few weeks but make a magnificent show during that time. The female flower usually stays a creamy yellow colour and is still most attractive, although not as spectacular as the male flower.

The shrub usually only grows to about 1.5 m in height and width. It has a bushy and reasonably dense habit if kept well trimmed. The flowers are carried on fairly short (approximately 30 cm) stems that are mostly branched. Each stem may carry 3–4 flowers on shorter side stems.

Even out of the flowering season the soft grey-green foliage of *L. discolor* makes it a very attractive garden plant.

L. discolor is a very easy protea to grow and will tolerate a wide range of climates and soil types. It is however reasonably frost tender while young, although damage is usually only to the new soft growth. Any open, sunny and well drained position in the garden should suit it.

L. discolor makes an excellent cut flower, however it usually only flowers for 2–3 weeks depending on weather conditions. It is also difficult to gain long stems, the multiple heads making it more suitable for posies or small vase arrangements. *L. discolor* is quite suitable for drying.

Leucadendron eucalyptifolium

One of the larger leucadendrons, *L. eucalyptifolium* makes a most attractive and useful windbreak or screening plant. Shrubs grow to approximately 6 m and up to 4 m across. As its name suggests the foliage is similar in appearance to that of the Australian eucalypt or gum tree, although much finer.

The leaves are a bright apple green, but the long bracts surrounding the smaller gold flower heads at the shoot tips turn bright gold in late winter or spring. Due to the very bushy nature of this plant it is a very spectacular sight when flowering, the whole shrub changing to a mass of gold.

It is also one of the few leucadendrons with a reasonably strong, but very pleasing scent.

L. eucalyptifolium is very easy to grow in most areas but must be kept well trimmed to prevent it becoming straggly and untidy with age.

The foliage is excellent for cut foliage all through the year and especially during the flowering season. The stems are slender and straight, making them ideal for any floral arrangement or floral art. This species also has quite a long vase life.

Leucadendron floridum

This smaller leucadendron has quite attractive silvery-green foliage and light yellow or lemon-coloured flowers in late spring. The shrub grows to a quite dense 1.5 m and is very compact in shape.

The flowers are clustered along the stem and make this an excellent leucadendron for cut foliage. The silver-green leaves and soft yellow flowers blend in beautifully with a wide variety of other flower colours and textures.

Although not commonly found in home gardens this leucadendron deserves far more attention than it presently gains. Its neat and compact shape and pleasant foliage make it an excellent landscaping plant. *L. floridum* has also proved quite easy to grow although it does require a reasonable amount of moisture during the drier months of the year. It is also reasonably frost tender while young. Young plants should be kept well trimmed to maintain compact shape.

Leucadendron gandogeri (Golden Glory)

This is a most outstanding and attractive leuca-dendron despite its rather ugly-sounding scientific name.

L. gandogeri grows to a bushy 1.5 to 2 m in height and produces beautiful rich golden-yellow bracts and flowers. The large leaves are normally a bright green with a tinge of red around their

borders for most of the year. However younger leaves may be totally copper red in colour at certain times of the year.

The large bracts around the flower head turn a rich golden-yellow colour in late winter and spring. These coloured bracts may be up to 70 mm in length making quite a large flower head. The flowers are usually single and terminal on long stems making *L. gandogeri* an ideal cut flower. The cut stems also have a long vase life.

L. gandogeri is very easy to grow and makes an excellent garden specimen plant or a low screening plant. It requires a well ventilated and open sunny position and should be kept well pruned to maintain its shape.

Although this is not a common garden plant it is highly recommended for its beautiful flowers and the ease with which it can be grown.

Leucadendron lanigerum

This spreading but very attractive leucadendron grows to about 1.5–2 m in height and up to 2 m in width.

One of the first leucadendrons to be widely grown in home gardens, *L. lanigerum* has fine, light green leaves which are quite dense along the stems. The end bracts turn a soft butter yellow in late winter and spring. Some variants develop a reddish tinge to the bracts as the flower ages on the plant.

The foliage is a very useful filler for floral work, the delicate flowers making it excellent for small posies or light open small vase arrangements.

One of the features of *L. lanigerum* is that it is one of the most hardy and easily grown species of the whole protea group. It tolerates heavy to sandy soils and is quite suitable for exposed coastal gardens. The spreading nature of the shrub also makes it ideal for low gardens and rockeries.

Leucadendron laureolum

This is another very attractive leucadendron that has been popular for many years with home gardeners and the cut flower industry.

The large yellow tulip-like flower heads are produced right through the winter months and make a beautiful show at a time of the year when most of the garden is quite dull.

The male flowers tend to develop a much

brighter yellow colour than the female ones which may only turn to a light lime green colour. The brightness of the flower also depends on the site the shrub is growing in. A much brighter bract colour develops in open sunny positions than in semi-shaded areas.

L. laureolum grows to about 2.5 m in height and width, and needs to be kept trimmed to prevent it becoming untidy. The coloured flower heads are born on almost every stem, making it a very prolific producer of cut flowers. The stems are usually straight and may grow to a length of 60-70 cm, ideal for larger vase or display-type arrangements. The cut stems have a long vase life.

Like most of the leucadendrons *L. laureolum* is easily grown in most well drained soils and is at its best colour-wise in open sunny sites. It is also quite disease and frost resistant. An excellent specimen shrub for all gardens, *L. laureolum* also makes an excellent windbreak or screening plant.

Leucadendron nervosum

This is a smaller compact leucadendron which features small light yellow flower heads. The inner bracts surrounding the flower itself have a covering of fine white hairs which give the flower head a most attractive soft frosted appearance.

The shrub only grows to a slender 1-1.5 m in height with long straight stems coming from the base of the shrub. The flowers appear in early spring. The leaves are almost oval and quite hard and stiff to touch.

L. nervosum is reasonably easy to cultivate and will tolerate moderate frosts. It makes an excellent garden plant especially when grown in a mixed garden bed. The shrubs need regular trimming to prevent them becoming untidy.

Leucadendron orientale ('Scented Petals')

This is a very interesting leucadendron with large elegant yellow or yellow and pink flower heads. *L. orientale* has very large, long, elegant leaves with a fine paper-like texture and often tinged with red or pink. The bracts surrounding the flower turn a golden yellow in mid-winter forming a large open flower head with a pleasant sweet scent. The central flower parts become quite sticky with nectar. The female flower heads often become blushed with red as the flower ages.

L. orientale grows to a compact 1.5 m in height with long straight stems extending from lower down on the main trunk. It should be kept neatly pruned to maintain a good shape and to encourage more flowering stems.

The combination of the long papery leaves tinged with colour and the large open flower head make *L. orientale* one of the most elegant leucadendrons. The long stems can be picked for cut foliage over a long period of time as even when not flowering they are most attractive.

L. orientale requires a well drained and sunny position and does not like to be crowded by other plants, which may cause it to become susceptible to fungal diseases.

L. orientale makes an excellent unusual cut flower and an interesting garden specimen plant, especially as it is quite different from many other leucadendrons.

Leucadendron procerum

A very attractive tall leucadendron, *L. procerum* may grow up to 3 m in height and 2 m in width. The small blue-green leaves and bushy branched habit make this an attractive shrub even when not in flower.

The flowers are produced in masses in late winter and spring, with the bracts surrounding the claret-coloured central flower parts turning a soft cream colour. Unfortunately the flowering parts become untidy after 2-3 weeks.

The masses of flowers make this a most useful cut flower for mixed commercial plantations as well as the home garden. *L. procerum* is relatively hardy and suitable for most garden situations where other proteas grow. It does require regular pruning to maintain its compact shape as the branches tend to droop if they become too long.

Leucadendron rubrum

This is a very unusual leucadendron in that it produces a large green cone-like flower head on the female plant. This green and later coppery brown cone looks a little like a protea flower bud before it opens. The female flower parts actually protrude in a small tuft from the tip of the green cones giving them a most unusual appearance. When the cone finally opens it takes on a fluffy brown appearance before the seeds are released.

The female plant, which is most commonly grown, reaches about 1.5 m in height and needs to be pruned while young to encourage a bushier growth habit. The flower buds appear in late winter and the cones develop right through spring to summer.

This is an unusual garden specimen plant and cones are often used in dried floral arrangements, retaining their coppery brown colouring. When the cones open (usually on a dead or fallen branch) the fluffy open flower heads are also very useful for dried arrangements.

Leucadendron salicifolium

This is a very large and vigorous leucadendron growing to over 3 m in height and 2–3 m in width. It produces masses of delicate yellow bracts in late winter or early spring. The flowers are produced in large numbers along each stem making a spectacular display.

L. salicifolium is very easily grown in all soil types and is quite fast growing. It is also resistant to most common diseases and pests. It makes an excellent windbreak or tall screening plant for the home garden and is widely grown by commercial growers, producing huge amounts of cut foliage per bush. The delicate bracts and soft cream-yellow colour make this a popular foliage with florists and floral artists. It can be used as both a filler in large display arrangements or in small posy or bowl arrangements.

L. salicifolium (male plants) produces masses of pollen which may make it unpopular with hay-fever sufferers. A very attractive and useful leucadendron if you have lots of space.

Leucadendron salignum

L. salignum in one of its many forms is probably one of the best known and most widely cultivated of all the protea-type plants. It varies in growth habit from a tall bushy shrub to low, prostrate, almost groundcover-type plants. The range of colours is almost as great. *L. salignum* can be found with bright red bracts through all shades of crimson to even pink tonings. There is also a large selection of cream through yellow to deep gold varieties.

The taller shrub variants of *L. salignum* usually grow to a maximum of 2.5 m in height and about 1.5–2 m in width. The stems are usually dark red with fine dark green, red-tinged leaves. The bracts change colour throughout the year. In autumn the new growth usually has a bright red colour which changes to deep red towards winter and may darken to almost dark green. As spring approaches the bracts surrounding the flower heads often become creamy-yellow or even autumn tones before returning to a red colour again towards summer.

The yellow or cream variants usually retain their yellow colourings for the whole season.

The smaller, lower-growing variants of *L. salignum* usually have finer foliage and some have almost linear leaves. The red colour types go through the same colour changes as the taller plants.

In all its varieties *L. salignum* is very easily grown in all soil types and climates. Depending on the variety you choose a suitable *L. salignum* could be found for almost every garden purpose or position.

The lovely fine foliage and delicate bracts make *L. salignum* extremely popular with floral artists and florists. It is widely grown for commercial purposes and is most popular because it can be picked and sold at almost any time of year.

Many varieties of *L. salignum* are currently being marketed under a huge range of nursery names which may become quite confusing. There are many cultivars and selections available to suit every garden purpose and your nurseryman should be consulted for advice.

Leucadendron sessile

This is another leucadendron which is not well known among gardeners but is well worth growing. *L. sessile* forms a lovely dense compact shrub to about 1.5–2 m in height and 1.5 m in width.

The male plant, which is the most commonly available, produces bright, butter yellow bracts surrounding a flat flower head about 25 mm in diameter.

The flowers are produced in late winter to early spring and often become tinged with red later in the flowering season. *L. sessile* flowers do not have great individual stem length but each stem usually carries several flowers making them still very useful as a cut flower. It does however have a relatively short vase life with the yellow bracts turning brown after several days.

L. sessile makes an excellent showy garden plant either as a single shrub or as part of a mixed garden. It is quite hardy and will even grow on heavier clay soils, but it does prefer some summer watering.

Leucadendron stroblinum

This is an excellent leucadendron both for the home gardener and the keen floral artist. Both the male and female plants produce masses of very desirable flowers on medium-sized compact shrubs.

The male *L. stroblinum* grows to about 2 × 2 m with masses of stems forming a lovely rounded shrub. The short rounded leaves are usually a bright green with the end bracts turning a beautiful bright gold in late winter and spring. The actual flower head forms a distinctive silvery-white round button shape fringed with yellow stamens.

The female *L. stroblinum* grows to about 1.5 m in height and can be quite spreading in habit. The leaves, stems and flowers of the female plant are much larger than those of the male. The flower bracts turn a light green often tinged with red and open to form a flower head up to 80 mm in diameter, revealing the small green cone in the centre. Female flowers are usually carried on quite long, thick stems up to 40 cm in length.

L. stroblinum makes an interesting and showy garden specimen and a useful cut flower. The male flowers do not have long stems but can be picked in clusters. *L. stroblinum* is easily cultivated in most well drained soils in an open sunny position.

Leucadendron thymifolium

As the name suggests this leucadendron has thyme-like foliage. The leaves are small and oval shaped, growing very closely along the slender stems. *L. thymifolium* grows to about 1.5 m in height and width and if not pruned heavily while young can tend to be quite a sparse shrub with several long erect main stems.

The flowers are quite small, only 10–15 mm in diameter, but are carried in clusters on the ends of the stems. The straw-yellow male flowers are almost daisy-like and appear in spring.

Female flowers are very small and barely noticeable but develop into attractive small pink cones.

L. thymifolium needs well drained sandy soils but will tolerate a heavier clay subsoil if well drained. It does not seem to be bothered by many common pests.

L. thymifolium makes an unusual garden specimen especially in a mixed protea garden. The flowers and cones are used by florists in smaller arrangements, however it is not widely grown by commercial growers.

Leucadendron tinctum (Rose Cockade)

This is one of the most widely cultivated leucadendrons. The female plant is easily recognised by its very large, open, rose red flowers which strongly resemble a large rosette.

The shrub tends to grow to a dense spreading 1.5 m in height and up to 2 m in width. *L. tinctum* does need to be kept well trimmed to prevent it becoming untidy as many stems tend to grow almost horizontal before turning upwards.

The leaves can be very large, up to 12 cm in length, and are quite papery giving the plant an elegant appearance. The flower bracts begin a light green colour and become blushed with red from the centre. After flowering a large dark red cone develops and the bracts darken to a deep claret red. The main flowering time is spring but the flowers remain attractive right through to mid-summer.

L. tinctum does require well drained soil and an open sunny site but is otherwise reasonably easy to grow. The large leaves are popular with flower spiders and may also be attacked by some leaf-eating insects.

L. tinctum has not been grown widely by commercial growers and is more commonly seen as a garden specimen plant. The flowers make an excellent show in any arrangement either as a feature flower or a filler. Finding long straight stems may sometimes be difficult.

Leucadendron uliginosum

This is a highly ornamental leucadendron with tall slender stems and quite unique silvery-grey foliage. *L. uliginosum* grows to a smallish rounded shrub of about 1.5 m in height but tends to have several tall slender stems which extend above the main part of the shrub. With careful pruning a more bushy shape can be developed.

The leaves are elliptical and only about 7–8 mm long. They are covered in very fine hairs which give the foliage its shiny silvery appearance.

Male flowers are like small cream stars at the ends of the longer stems and contrast beautifully with the silvery-grey foliage. The cream bracts surround a small butter-yellow central flower mass. The flowers appear mainly in spring through to early summer.

L. uliginosum has been grown for commercial purposes for many years. The delicate foliage and flowers make excellent filling material and are very popular with both florists and floral artists. The foliage is in demand throughout the year, not just at flowering time. This leucadendron makes an excellent interesting garden specimen.

L. uliginosum requires a well drained sunny position and is quite resistant to most common diseases and pests.

Leucadendron xanthaconus

The most commonly grown form is the female plant which has masses of small yellow flowers along long stems.

L. xanthaconus grows to a large shrub of approximately 3 m in height and 2.5 m in width. It should be kept heavily trimmed to prevent it from becoming straggly with age.

In mid-spring the flower bracts turn from light green to a bright yellow in masses along the long straight stems. These then develop into clusters of very attractive pink-red cones.

L. xanthaconus is a popular foliage with florists either when in flower or in the cone stage. It makes an excellent windbreak or screening plant for the large garden or commercial plantations. It is a vigorous and fast-growing plant and is easily grown in most well drained soils.

Leucadendron 'Silvan Red' (hybrid)

This outstanding hybrid leucadendron has proved to be extrmely popular both with the home gardener and commercial growers.

L. 'Silvan Red' was developed by Proteaflora Enterprises Pty Ltd from Silvan, Australia and is a hybrid cross between *L. salignum* and *L. laureolum*. It has many outstanding qualities, including the best attributes of both parent plants.

'Silvan Red' grows to about 2 m in height and 1.5 m in width in most soils. It is quite fast growing and will usually develop a good dense compact shape even without pruning.

The leaves are dark green tinged with red on attractive red stems. The flowering bracts develop in early autumn when they are a beautiful bright red, but as autumn progresses to winter the colour gradually deepens to a rich deep red. Over the cooler winter months the bracts may take on a dark greenish appearance before gradually becoming lighter. During spring they soften in colour through a lovely range of reds and pinks or even autumn tonings.

The flowers are carried on stems up to 1.2 m in length and can be picked for almost 12 months of the year, especially if pruning times on different plants are varied.

'Silvan Red' is extremely hardy, growing in almost all soils and climates. It will tolerate all but the heaviest of frosts and is resistant to most of the common diseases.

'Silvan Red' is an outstanding garden plant for a variety of uses, and makes a striking feature plant, garden windbreak or screen. It has also been used as a spectacular garden hedge as it responds well to harsh pruning.

Commercial growers have been growing 'Silvan Red' for many years in large quantities. It is extremely popular on the export market where the main requirement is long (up to 1 m) straight stems and unblemished blooms.

'Silvan Red' is used extensively by florists and floral artists in all types of arrangements. It also dries extremely well and is a most useful flower in dried floral work. It is noted for an extremely long vase life especially if the vase water is changed every few days.

Leucadendron 'Safari Sunset' (hybrid)

L. 'Safari Sunset' is a cross from the same parents as *L.* 'Silvan Red', that is, *L. laureolum* × *L. salignum*.

It was first developed in New Zealand and is grown extensively there for the export trade. 'Safari Sunset' is very similar to 'Silvan Red', but the flowers and leaves are slightly thicker and larger. Also 'Safari Sunset' usually has deeper, darker tonings than 'Silvan Red'.

'Safari Sunset' grows to approximately 2 × 2 m and forms a dense rounded shrub.

The flowers develop from autumn onwards and usually start off a rich claret red. They then go through a colour change similar to that of 'Silvan Red' through the winter months to spring. The range of autumn tones, pinks and reds through this period makes this leucadendron a most interesting and attractive garden plant and extremely popular for cut flowers. Like 'Silvan Red', 'Safari Sunset' has an extremely long vase life, lasting up to two months in clean water.

'Safari Sunset' is very hardy and easy to grow in all situations and is highly recommended for all gardens.

Leucadendron 'Red Devil' (*L. salignum* cultivar)

L. 'Red Devil' is a selected cultivar of *L. salignum*. This is only one of a huge range of selected cultivars of *L. salignum* becoming available through the nursery industry. They all have very similar requirements for cultivation. 'Red Devil' grows to about 1 m in height and 1 m in width and forms a spreading shrub with upright stems.

The fine foliage is a pleasing blue-grey and the smallish flowers range from soft shades of pink or rose through to lovely deep pinkish-crimson colourings. The flower bracts develop in autumn and change colour through winter to spring in a similar manner to the standard *L. salignum*.

'Red Devil' is a very hardy cultivar and will grow in almost any open sunny situation. It is also quite frost hardy.

It makes an excellent cut flower, the delicate flowers and colours making it perfect for posies and bouquets. Stem length can be up to 50 cm but most tend to be less than 40 cm. This cultivar has an extremely long vase life.

'Red Devil' is an ideal plant for many garden situations such as rockeries, low gardens or even in a mixed cottage garden. It does not seem to be grown in large quantities for commercial purposes but certainly has commercial prospects.

Leucadendron 'Yellow Crest' (*L. salignum* cultivar)

L. 'Yellow Crest' is one of a large number of selected yellow cultivars of *L. salignum*. Many of these are virtually identical but have been given different nursery names by the propagating nurseries.

'Yellow Crest' grows to approximately 1 m in height and width forming a neat rounded shrub. It should be kept well trimmed in the first few years to encourage denser growth. The bright yellow terminal flowers develop during winter and persist for a long period on the shrub.

'Yellow Crest' is very hardy grown on most well drained soils and is quite frost hardy. It makes an excellent feature plant due to its striking colour and blends well with most other plant types. The flowers are usually carried on stems up to 50 cm long and are excellent long-lasting cut flowers.

This cultivar is grown mainly as a garden plant but certainly has commercial potential.

Leucadendron 'Maui Sunset' (hybrid)

This is an outstanding hybrid leucadendron only recently gaining recognition world wide. It was first developed in Hawaii and is thought to be a cross between *L. laureolum* and either *L. salignum* or *L. discolor*.

L. 'Maui Sunset' grows to approximately 2 m in height with a quite upright habit. The flowers develop in late winter through to early spring. The bracts are usually a yellow-white colour tinged with light-green and crimson. They open to form a flower up to 80 mm in diameter. The stem length is not as long as in most of the larger leucadendrons being on average 30-40 cm.

'Maui Sunset' has proved to be very hardy and frost resistant in most soils but testing in many different soil types is still required. Careful pruning while the plant is young is needed to promote bushy growth.

'Maui Sunset' makes an excellent larger garden shrub and certainly has huge commercial potential.

Genus *Leucospermum*

Leucospermum catherinae (Catherine Wheel)

This is a very interesting leucospermum which has been common in cultivation for many years. It is easily indentified by the distinctive way in which the styles point around in a circle, giving the flower its Catherine wheel appearance.

L. catherinae grows to a spreading 2 m in height and up to 2.5 m in width. It generally forms quite a dense rounded shrub but does need regular pruning to maintain a neat appearance.

The large leaves are blue-grey with the distinctive red points of the genus. They have a distinctive parchment or papery feel to them and are densely packed along the stems.

The flowers are up to 18 cm in diameter and are usually a light pink-orange or pink-gold. They are usually carried on long stems to 45 cm. The main flowering time is early spring through to early summer and the onset of warmer weather finishes the flowers fairly quickly.

L. catherinae is quite hardy given reasonable drainage and an open sunny position. It is reasonably frost tender while young but older established plants will rarely be troubled.

As one of the larger leucospermum species *L. catherinae* makes an excellent feature plant in any garden. Its extended flowering time and larger flowers give an excellent show over a longer period of time than many of the other leucospermums.

Although popular with florists and floral artists *L. catherinae* is not commonly grown in large quantities for commercial purposes.

Leucospermum conocarpodendron

L. conocarpodendron has been used extensively by the nursery trade to produce some beautiful hybrid leucospermums. It grows to a large rounded shrub of 2 m. The large glossy green leaves are strongly toothed with yellow or orange tips.

The flowers form a compact ball approximately 80 mm in diameter. The usual colour is a bright yellow-gold with the main flowering time usually coinciding with the first hot weather of late spring or early summer.

L. conocarpodendron requires an open, well drained site and once established is quite hardy. Severe frosts may cause problems especially while the plant is young and it may need some frost protection then. Careful pruning while the plant is young will also help produce a neater adult plant.

Its strong, dark green, glossy leaves and compact shape make *L. conocarpodendron* an excellent garden shrub which also produces a spectacular show when in flower. It would be equally useful as a border plant or a feature in an open area or lawn.

L. conocarpodendron's striking colour and compact flower head make it ideal for floral art or floristry work. It has been grown commercially for a number of years both for export and local sale. The flowers are very long lasting once picked and also transport well.

Leucospermum cordifolium

L. cordifolium is probably the best known leucospermum species. It has also been used extensively with many other species to produce some excellent hybrid leucospermums.

In its natural habitat in southern Africa *L. cordifolium* is found in a vast range of soil types and climates. This variety of habitats has produced a huge range of growth habits, leaf types and flower colours within the species. Many of these regional types have been selected by the nursery industry and selectively propagated for certain distinctive characteristics. When selecting a cultivar for your particular garden ask for advice from your nurseryman.

L. cordifolium commonly grows to a spreading open shrub of 1.5 m height and 2 m width. There are, however, selected cultivars which are almost prostrate groundcovers and others with a much taller or more upright growth habit.

The flowers are a flattened ball shape usually about 75–100 mm in diameter. Cultivar colours range from light yellow through oranges, light red, pink and apricot to a deep red. The strong red colourings are the most popular on the international market.

The leaves are usually quite small and light green but this again varies greatly between cultivars. Leaf shape and size may even vary in the same shrub.

Generally *L. cordifolium* is the easiest of the common leucospermums to cultivate. It can tolerate a wide range of soils from sandy to gravel or even clay. The main requirement is good drainage for most of the year. An open sunny position is important for good flower production, as semi-shaded plants tend to produce fewer blooms of a paler colour.

L. cordifolium is reasonably frost hardy once established, however young plants should be protected in severe frosts. Susceptibility to certain fungal diseases has caused problems in some commercial plantations but recently most selections have been made from resistant plant stock. Chewing insects sometimes attack the leaves but this rarely results in plant death. Grasshoppers have been a problem in some areas.

Due to the large range of selected cultivars gardeners should be able to find a variety of *L. cordifolium* which suits their particular purpose and climate.

L. cordifolium has been the most widely commercially grown leucospermum for many years and has remained extremely popular on the international market. The main preference has been for the cultivars with clear, strong colours and long straight stems.

Leucospermum cuneiforme

A lovely bushy shrub which grows to about 2 × 2 m, *L. cuneiforme* produces bright, light yellow flowers in late spring and early summer.

It requires very well drained lighter soils and full sun. It is reasonably frost tender and may require protection from severe frosts.

L. cuneiforme makes an excellent garden plant with its compact habit and showy yellow flowers. It has not been cultivated commercially in large numbers.

Leucospermum gerradii

A very low-growing leucospermum which rarely grows to more than 0.75 m in height, *L. gerradii* produces large yellow-orange flowers in late spring. The styles are fairly sparse but this species has very prominent perianths which are usually yellow striped with red, making it a quite distinctive and attractive flower.

L. gerradii does require very good drainage and is reasonably frost tender. An excellent, interesting specimen plant for the smaller garden.

Leucospermum glabrum

One of the largest plants of the *Leucospermum* genus, *L. glabrum* grows to a large shrub 2.5–3 m high and approximately 1.5 m in wide.

It produces large flowers up to 100 mm in diameter in late spring and early summer. The prominant styles are relatively short and thick, giving the overall flower an almost spherical shape. The styles are usually yellow or orange and the perianths a vivid red with a white fringe.

These spectacular flowers and the large thick glossy leaves make *L. glabrum* an extremely attractive shrub.

L. glabrum has been used frequently by the nursery industry to produce some very beautiful hybrid species.

It has shown itself to be adaptable to many different soil types and climates and is more frost resistant than most other leucospermums.

L. glabrum makes an outstanding large feature shrub for the larger home garden. The distinct colours and strong dark green foliage make it a popular cut flower.

Leucospermum lineare

This is an interesting leucospermum in that it has very long thin, almost linear leaves which produce a shrub very different in appearance from all other leucospermums.

L. lineare grows to a compact 2 m in height with a quite slender erect habit. The long straight stems usually extend in masses from the main trunk lower in the bush.

The flower colour may vary from a fairly insipid light orange through to bright red. The more distinctive colour forms have tended to be the varieties selected for cultivation in recent years. The flowers are produced earlier than those of most other leucospermums, from early spring.

L. lineare is quite easily cultivated and fairly frost hardy, unlike many of the other members of this genus. It is also quite disease resistant. Regular pruning will produce masses of flowering stems.

L. lineare makes a lovely compact garden shrub and an excellent addition to any leucospermum collection on account of its earlier flowering season. The long slender stems make it an ideal cut flower for all types of arrangements. It has not been grown widely commercially, probably due to lack of availability of the varieties with the more distinctive flower colours.

Leucospermum patersonii

A large shrub or small tree, *L. patersonii* grows to approximately 3.5 m. The bright orange flowers are produced from early spring through to early summer. The leaves are large and dark green and deeply toothed, with the characteristic red points.

L. patersonii requires very good drainage and its distinctive feature is that it is one of the few proteas which will grow in alkaline soils, its natural habitat in South Africa being limestone-rich coastal areas.

This is an excellent specimen plant especially for those gardeners who cannot grow other protea species due to strongly alkaline soils.

Leucospermum reflexum (Red Rocket, Sky Rocket, Yellow Rocket, *L. luteum*)

L. reflexum has been a widely cultivated and very popular garden plant for many years. The lower rows of styles straighten and point downwards to give the flower its very characteristic sky rocket or comet-like appearance.

L. reflexum may grow up to 4 × 4 m in size and makes a spectacular show when in full bloom. The flowers are quite large and produced on very long stems to 60 cm. The main flowering time is spring to early summer.

The most common varieties are a bright flame-red colour. An attractive bright yellow variety is also available. Its correct name is *L. reflexum* var. *luteum*, however it is often sold as *L.* 'Yellow Rocket' or, more incorrectly, *L. luteum*.

The leaves are an attractive soft grey colour and are quite small and narrow, growing close to the stems.

L. reflexum has been cultivated for the commercial market for a number of years. The long straight stems, attractive foliage, bright distinctive flowers and long vase life make it an ideal cut flower for the florist trade. It is a spectacular garden plant for those with enough space.

Leucospermum tottum (Pink Star)

One of the few leucospermums to develop a true pink colour, *L. tottum* grows to a spreading shrub approximately 1.5 m in height and up to 2 m in width. The stems, especially the outer ones, tend to branch greatly and grow horizontally, with the flower heads at right angles to the stem.

The flowers appear from early spring through to early summer and are most commonly a soft pink with deeper crimson centres. The outer rows of styles open almost horizontal giving the flower a delicate star-like appearance.

L. tottum requires very well drained acid soils and an open sunny site. It is quite frost tender while growing and moderately sensitive when fully grown.

The delicate pink flowers make this an attractive garden plant. The 'bent' nature of the flowers make it difficult to use as a cut flower but the longer straight stems from the centre of the shrub would be useful. The cut flowers have a long vase life.

L. tottum has been used as a parent in several very useful and attractive hybrids by the wholesale nursery industry.

Leucospermum 'Firewheel' (hybrid)

One of the early hybrids produced from *L. cordifolium*, *L.* 'Firewheel' has proved to be an extremely hardy and fast-growing leucospermum. It grows to about 2 × 2 m forming a dense compact shrub. The masses of stems produce an enormous number of blooms each year, the shrub being virtually completely hidden by the light-orange blooms in late spring.

'Firewheel' develops long straight stems and has been used extensively by florists. The only criticism of this leucospermum is that the flower colours tend not to be distinctive enough, especially for the export industry. Also the flower heads tend to break off the stems quite easily making them difficult to transport.

'Firewheel' makes an outstanding fast-growing garden plant and is extremely easy to grow in most areas.

Leucospermum 'Calypso' (hybrid)

A beautiful hybrid leucospermum produced from a cross between *L. cordifolium* and *L. glabrum*, *L.* 'Calypso' grows to approximately 1.5 × 1.5 m forming a neat compact shrub.

The flowers are produced from mid-spring through to early summer. They have bright orange styles with bright pink perianths underneath and are up to approximately 75 mm in diameter.

The large dark green leaves and dense habit make 'Calypso' an attractive garden shrub. It has also proved very hardy and easy to grow in most well drained soils. This hybrid is quite frost hardy and resistant to most fungal diseases which affect leucospermums. An open sunny position will promote flower production.

'Calypso' makes an excellent border shrub or a neat compact feature plant in a lawn or open area. The flowers have a very long vase life and are carried on long straight stems.

Leucospermum 'Scarlet Ribbon' (hybrid)

This leucospermum hybrid has been produced from a cross between L. glabrum and L. tottum. L. 'Scarlet Ribbon' grows to approximately 1.5 × 1.5 m forming a round compact shrub.

The scarlet red flowers are produced in late spring and the perianths have a slight white fringe (like the L. glabrum parent) giving the flower a slightly 'frosted' appearance.

'Scarlet Ribbon' grows on most well drained, acid soils and requires full sun. It has also proved quite frost hardy once established.

The distinctive colours and long vase life make 'Scarlet Ribbon' an excellent cut flower. It is also an excellent hardy garden shrub.

Leucospermum 'Mardi Gras' (hybrid)

This is a spectacular hybrid between L. conocarpodendron and L. glabrum.

The ball-shaped flowers have shortish thick, bright orange or gold styles. The perianths below are striped mainly with red and orange and fringed with a white beard. The overall effect of a riot of bright colour make this one of the most brilliant leucospermum hybrids.

L. 'Mardi Gras' rarely exceeds 1.5 m in height, forming a neat compact shrub. It grows very easily in most well drained spots and a sunny position is necessary to produce the best blooms.

This hybrid is an outstanding addition to any garden as either a border plant or main feature. The cut flowers last well although stem length is often less than 30 cm.

Genus Serruria

Serruria florida ('Blushing Bride')

A very beautiful member of the Protea Family which has become extremely popular in recent years, S. florida or 'Blushing Bride' has been most sought after by florists, especially for use in bridal bouquets.

'Blushing Bride' grows to a straggly 1.5 m in height if left unpruned. In cultivation and with careful pruning it rarely grows to more than 1 m. Garden specimens rarely become attractive, compact shrubs but the outstanding flowers make growing 'Blushing Bride' well worthwhile.

The small compact flowers are made up of 3-4 rows of snow-white papery bracts surrounding a tuft-like central flower mass. Both the central flower mass and the bracts become blushed with pink giving the flower its characteristic delicate colourings. The pink blushing seems to relate to bruising or movement of the flower. Plants grown in very sheltered conditions produce mostly white flowers with little pink blushing.

Blooms are produced through winter to early spring and may be carried as single or multiple flowers on each stem.

'Blushing Bride' has proved to be very unreliable in cultivation. It is notorious for growing well for a long time and then suddenly dying for no apparent reason. However, with a little extra care and by following a few simple rules most gardeners should be able to successfully grow their own 'Blushing Bride'.

'Blushing Bride' requires very well drained, acid soils, sandy loams probably being the best. It also requires a position in full sun and is quite frost sensitive, especially in the first two years. Serrurias also resent rich soils so fertilisers are not required.

Although 'Blushing Bride' requires good drainage, it also seems that it cannot withstand long dry periods. Light watering during the drier months is required.

'Blushing Bride' requires continual tip pruning in the first two years to encourage a busy compact shape, otherwise it tends to grow two or three long straggly main stems. Care must also be taken not to over prune as this will often kill the plant, even when it is quite large.

If a bushy denser type of shrub can be grown 'Blushing Bride' makes a beautiful garden feature. Its main value, however, is for the floral artist. 'Blushing Bride' is grown extensively for the local florist trade and the blooms always command a premium price at wholesale markets. It has excellent lasting qualities after picking and is ideal for bouquets and posies.

Glossary

acid   Substance which has a pH value of less than 7.

alkali   Substance which neutralises acids and has a pH value of greater than 7.

bract   A modified leaf, generally coloured, which forms part of the protea flower head.

cambium   The outer layer of plant stems, under which the sap-carrying vessels lie.

cultivar   A variety of plant selected for some special feature, e.g. colour. Selected cultivars are often given special nursery names and must be registered internationally. They have usually been propagated by cutting from an attractive freak variation of one of the standard species.

dibber   A small stick with one pointed end used to create holes in potting mix for transplanting seedlings

flower mass   Usually describes the true flower parts of the protea. This is the central part of the flower head and is actually a mass of individual florets.

floret   An individual flower that is part of a compound flower.

foliar   Of or belonging to the foliage.

fungicide   Chemical used to control or kill fungus.

genus   Part of the classification system. This group contains a number of species, e.g. *Protea* (genus) *repens* (species).

hybrid   Plant produced from a cross between two *different* species. Hybrids are noted for their vigorous and hardy nature.

insecticide   Chemical used to control or kill insects.

lignotuber   A swelling at the base of the stem which forms an underground trunk. It contains dormant buds and is an adaptation to fire. The buds shoot after loss of stems.

linear   Very narrow or needle-like.

miticide   Chemical used to control or kill mites.

perianth   The envelope outside the stamens. This is often very colourful and ribbon-like in leucospermums.

pollen   Small particles containing the male gamete released from male flower parts.

protea   The general name given to members of the plant tribe Proteae which includes the genera *Protea, Leucadendron, Leucospermum, Serruria, Aulux, Mimetes* and others.

scale   Flat, scale-like, sap-sucking insect.

scarification   Any method used to break down the outer seed coat to help with germination.

semi-hardwood   The last season's growth which has hardened off; flexible but firm wood.

species   The smallest group in the classification system. Organisms within a species consistently show many characteristics in common.

stigma   The swollen, sticky top of the style which receives pollen.

style   The slender stalk which supports the stigma. These are very prominent in leucospermums, giving them their 'pin-cushion' appearance.

terminal   (Of flowers) carried at the tip of the stem.

transpiration   Loss of water from leaves and stems due to evaporation.

vegetative   (Of propagation) achieved using parts of the plant other than seed, e.g. cuttings.

Index